Table of Contents

Who should read this book?

Chapter 1-The Object-Oriented Programming Approach

Programming Models:

Procedural Programming

Object-Oriented Programming

Component-Based Model

Object-Orientation:

Object-Oriented Analysis and Design (OOAD)

Advantages of Object-Orientation

Chapter 2 – Fundamentals of Java   5..6

History of Java, Features of Java

JDK Tools: The javac Compiler, The java Interpreter, The appletviewer, The jdb Tool

The javap Disassemble, The Javadoc Tool, The javah Tool.

Chapter 3 – Introduction to Java Programming   7..27

Keywords

Data Types: Primitive data types, Abstract or Derived Data types

Variables: Variable naming Conventions, Variable Initialization,

Assigning values to variables

Literals:

Operators: Arithmetic Operators, Assignment Operators, Unary Operators

Comparison Operators, Shift Operators, The new Operator

Order of Precedence of Operators:

Type Conversion (Casting):

Decision Constructs:

The if .. else Construct

The switch Construct

Looping Constructs:

The while Loop

The do.. while Loop

The for Loop

Arrays: Single-Dimensional Arrays, Two-Dimensional Arrays

Chapter 4: Classes   28..48

Declaring a Class, Comment Entries, Naming Classes, Creating an Object

Data Members: Declaring Data Members, Indentation, Naming variables

Methods: Declaring Methods, Naming Methods

Using Class Members:

Using Data Members, Invoking a Methods, Passing Arguments to a Method

Constructors:

Access Specifiers:

> The public Access Specifier.
> The private Access Specifier.
> The protected Access Specifier.
> Default Access.

Modifiers: The static Modifiers, The final Modifiers.

Abstract Classes: The native Modifier, The transient Modifier.

Chapter 5: **Exception Handling** 49..56

Exceptions, Exception-Handling Techniques, User-Define Exceptions, Common Exceptions.

Chapter 6: Java Programs 57..63
> Applets and Applications.

Chapter 7: Using AWT in Applications 64-75
> User Interface, Components, Containers, Components and Controls, Menu.

Chapter 8: Event-Handling 76-82
> Events, Event-driven Programming, Handling an Event, Handling Window Events, Adapter Classes, Inner Classes.

Chapter 9: Networking 83-91

Overview of Sockets, IP addresses and Port, creating a socket, Importing Packages.

Chapter 10: Java Database Connectivity 92-105

Establishing a Connection (JDBC, ODBC connectivity), transactions with database.

About this Book

This book aims at imparting expertise in application development using java. You will learn to write applications using version 8 of the Java Development Kit (JDK 8). As part of this book, you will create classes, build GUI applications and applets, and implement even-handling, database connectivity, and TCP/IP sockets.

Who should Read this book

This book can be read by anyone who has an interest in object-oriented programming and is aspiring to become a Java programmer. If you are learning Java for the first time or working on Java-based application development and want to enhance your understanding of the subject, this book is for you.

This book provides a variety of examples and illustrations aimed at ensuring effective learning.

Chapter 1: The Object-Oriented Programming Approach

Objectives:

> In this Chapter, you will learn about:

> - ➤ Programming models
> - ➤ Procedural Programming
> - ➤ Object-Oriented Programming
> - ➤ Component-based programming
> - ➤ Object-Oriented Analysis and design
> - ➤ Classes and Objects

Programming Models:

The process of problem-solving using a computer is an intricate process requiring much through, careful planning, logical precision, persistence, and attention to details. On the other hand, it can be challenging, exciting, and satisfying with considerable scope for personal creativity and expression. If problems-solving is approached in the latter spirit, the chances of success are greatly amplified.

A programmer's primary task is to write software to solve a problem. Many programming models have evolved to help programmers in being more effective. These are briefly discussed below:

Procedural Programming:

The one way of solving a problem is to break is down into smaller parts and solve each of the smaller problems. Then, aggregate(collate) the solutions to solve the overall problem. Think of each small solution as a task, to perform which you write a block of code called a function. You can call one function from another. However, you must ensure that a function used to change one part of the system does not have an undesirable effect on another part of the system.

This approach to software development is process-centric or procedural since it looks at the procedures in a system. Such an approach is not ideally suited for developing complex software because it concentrates on the process of the application for which the software is being developed. The reusability of software becomes difficult as its complexity increases with processes.

Object-Oriented Programming:

An object is one of the first things that an infant learns to recognise. The multitude of 'things' that hover above its crib, that smile and talk to it, that pat its head and pinch its cheeks are people. Sometime later, it learns to recognise other such 'things' – the circular 'things' with a dial on one wall of the house is a clock, the longish 'things' arranged nearly on the shelves are books, and the wired contraption resting on the table and making a noise is the stereo sound system. Mind you, the infants do not know that these things are named so, but recognise them in much the same way as it recognises its mother and father.

As the infant grows older, it learns to recognise an object as not only having a definite, distinct boundary, but also as something that has a unique identity, quite apart from the other objects surrounding it.

An object has the following characteristics:

- o It has a state
- o It may display a behaviour
- o It has a unique identity

The state of an object is indicated by a set of attributes and the values of these attributes. Thus, a chemical compound can be characterised by its temperature, pressure, and density, and the values of each of these attributes.

The behaviour refers to a change of these attributes over a period of time.

Each object has a unique identity, just as each person has a unique identity. Thus, two tennis balls may be of the same colour and material, have the same weight and circumference, and display the same behaviour but still have distinct identities. Say, one ball has the factory seal number 'AS1234' and the other 'PN1234'.

Component-Based Model:

A component is a reusable software that can be easily plugged in or unplugged from man application. It uses the basics of object-oriented programming. In a component-based system, component interact with each other by calling methods and passing data.

So how the component-based model is is different from object-oriented programming?

The component-based model is a software architecture that allows applications and systems to be built from components supplied by different software vendors. It is a set of standards that allows any software to communicate with other software regardless of the hardware, the operating system and the programming language used for the development. It ensures that there is a standard method of interaction between the components. All objects need to follow these standards when providing functionality.

The model is a specification, which defines how components can communicate with each other. Component objects can be implemented in a number of programming language.

The component-based model is revisited in Section 20: RMI (Remote Method Invocation).

OBJECT-ORIENTATION:

Object-Oriented Analysis and Design (OOAD)

Imagine an aircraft factory in which a new jetliner is being built. Picture several component engineers and workers with specialised tools, constructing a marvel of technology. Can you visualise them working on pure intuition – grabbing the tools and settling down to work immediately? Or, do you see them working according to an elaborate design on which they have spent hours – pouring over each detail, working and re-working the design, and finally constructing the aircraft based on the design?

The same holds true for almost any item that is constructed. Fashion designers, for instance, put pen to paper before attacking the fabric with sessors. Architects spend hours drawing up blueprints before laying the bricks.

So, why should the construction of software be any different?

It is this 'paper-and-pencil' approach that is termed *analysis* and *design*. When we *analyse* and design a system, we build a model of the system. The purpose of this model is to help us understands the reality that we are trying to create. This model is simpler that the system that is finally constructed. Not all the practical aspects of building a system for the real world can be reflected in the design. However, this does not undermine the importance of design.

We need to distinguish between the stages of analysis and design. The analysis phase considers the system as a solution to a problem in its environment or domain. Broadly speaking, analysis is the stage in which the users and developers of the system arrive at a common understanding of the system. After all, a software professional cannot be expected to know the intricacies involved in air traffic scheduling. Similarly, airport personnel are not expected to know the syntax of programming languages. In order to build software for air traffic scheduling, both the software professionals and the airport personnel must speak the same language in terms of the problem domain.

The work of software professionals in the design stage is comparable to the work of an architect or a fashion designer. The designer generates a blueprint of the system that is to be implemented. In this stage, the developers of the system document their understanding of the system.

Advantages of Object-Orientation

Why do we opt for the object-oriented approach? The principal reasons are:

- Realistic Modelling
- Reusability
- Resilience to change

Realistic Modelling:

Since we live in a world of objects, it logically follows that the object-oriented approach models the real world more accurately than the conventional, procedural approach.

Reusability:

In the software industry, as in other industries, a large portion of time and energy is being spent in re-creating the proverbial wheel. In the object-oriented approach, you build classes, which can then be used by several applications.

The benefit of reusability translates to a saving in time and effort, which in turn results in cost benefits.

Resilience to change:

Through the object-oriented approach, systems can be allowed to evolve. When a change is suggested, the old system need not be completely abandoned and rebuilt from scratch. Resilience to change results in case of maintenance. For the same reason, even during construction, parts of the system under development can be refined without any major change to other parts.

CLASSES AND OBJECTS:

An object has state, exhibits some well-defined behaviour, and has a unique identity.

The state and behaviour together comprise the properties of an object. For example, one property of the object pre-paid mobile phone could be the amount of money or the re-charge plan.

Behaviour is how an object acts and reacts, in terms of its state changes and message passing. Objects do not exist in isolation. They interact with other objects and react to these interactions. These interactions take place through messages.

Two objects may have the same behaviour, may or may not have the same state but will never have the same identity. The identity of an object never changes in its lifetime.

A Class:

Classes and Objects are closely linked. You cannot consider one without the other. While an object has a unique identity, a class is an abstraction of the common properties of many objects.

A class is a set of attributes and behaviours shared by similar objects.

An object is not a class. A property of an object is not a class. Objects that do not share a common structure or common behaviour cannot be clubbed together in a class.

In the object-oriented approach, besides identifying objects and classes, the developer also has to define the structure of the class. This structure determines how the set of objects provides the behaviour needed to satisfy the requirement of the problem domain.

Chapter 2:   Fundamentals of Java

HISTORY OF JAVA:

Although the Java programming language is usually associated with the *world wideweb*, its origin predates the Web. Java began life as the programming language **Oak**.

Oak was developed by the members of the Green Project, which included Patrick Naughton, Mike Sheridan, and James Gosling, a group formed in 1991 to create products for the smart electronic market.

The team wanted a fundamentally new way of computing, based on the power networks, and wanted the same software to run on different kinds of computers, consumer gadgets and other devices. Patenting issues gave a new name to **Oak**- "**Java**".

During that period, Mosaic, the first graphical browser, was released. Non-programmers started accessing the World Wide Web and the Web grew dramatically. Very soon, Java become an integral part of the Web.

Java software works just about everywhere, from the smallest devices to supercomputers. Java technology components (programs) do not depend on the kind of computer, telephone, television, or operating system they run on. They work on any kind of compatible device that supports the Java platform.

FEATURES OF JAVA:

Java is a simple language that can be learned easily, even if you just started programming.

A Java programmer need not know the internals of Java. The syntax of java is smaller to C++. Unlike C++, in which the programmer handles memory manipulation, Java handles the required memory manipulation, and thus prevents error that arise due to improper memory usage.

Java defines data as objects with methods that support the objects. Java is purely object-oriented and provides abstraction, encapsulation, inheritance, and polymorphism. Even the most basic program has a class. Any code that you write in java is inside a class.

Java is tuned to the Web. Java programs can access data across the Web as easily as they access data from a local system. You can build distributed applications in Java that use resources from any other networked computer.

Java is both *interpreted* and *compiled*. The code to a *bytecode* that is binary and platform-independent. When the program has to be executed, the code is fetched into the memory and interpreted on the user's machine. As an interpreted language, java has simple syntax.

When you compile a piece of code, all the errors are listed together. You can execute a program only when all the errors have been rectified. An interpreter, on the other hand, verifies the code and executes it line by line. Only when the execution reaches the statement with an error is the error reported. This makes it easy for a programmer to debug the code. The drawback is that this takes more time than compilation.

Compilation is the process of converting the code that you type, into a language that the computer understands-machine language. When you compile a program using a compiler, the compiler checks for syntactical (grammatical) errors in code and list all the errors on the screen. You have to rectify the errors and recompile the program to get the matching language code. The Java compiler compiles the code to a *bytecode* that is understood by the Java environment.

Bytecode is the result of compiling a Java program. You can execute this code on any platform. In other words, due to the bytecode compilation process and interpretation by a browser, java programs can be executed on a variety of hardware and operating systems. The only requirement is that the system should have a Java-enabled Internet browser. The Java compiler is written in Java and the run-time environment, the interpreter, is written in C. The Java interpreter can execute java code directly on any machine on which a java interpreter has been installed.

Thanks to the *bytecode*, a Java program can run on any machine that has a Java interpreter. The bytecode supports connection to multiple databases. Java code is portable. Therefore, other people can use the programs that you write in Java even if they have different machines with different Operating Systems.

Multithreading is the ability of an application to perform multiple tasks at the same time. For example, when you play a game on your computer, on task of the program is to handle sound effects and another to handle screen display. A single program accomplishes many tasks simultaneously. Microsoft Word is another multithreading program in which the data is automatically saved as you key it in. You can create multithreading programs using Java. The core of Java is also multithreaded.

The following definition of Java by Sun Microsystems lists all the feature of Java:

'*Java is a simple, object-oriented, distributed, interpreted, robust, secure, architecture neutral, portable, high-performance, multithreaded, and dynamic language*'.

Chapter 3: INTRODUCTION TO JAVA PROGRAMMING:

In this Chapter you will learn about:

> ➢ JDK tools.
> ➢ Java Keywords.
> ➢ Data Types in java.
> ➢ Variable naming conventions.
> ➢ Initialising variables.
> ➢ Literals.
> ➢ Operators.
> ➢ Type Conversion.
> ➢ Decision constructs.
> ➢ Looping construct.
> ➢ Arrays

JDK Tools:

Java Development Toolkit (JDK) is a software package from Sun Microsystems. Regarding Oracle Java SE Support Roadmap, version 21 is the latest one, and versions 21, 17, 11 and 8 are the currently supported *long-term support* (LTS) versions, where Oracle Customers will receive Oracle Premier Support. Oracle continues to release no-cost public Java 8 updates for development and personal use indefinitely. Oracle also continues to release no-cost public Java 17 LTS updates for all users, including commercial and production use until September 2024.

The javac Compiler:

You can create Java programs using any text editor. The file you create should have the extension .java. Every file that you create (Source code) can have a maximum of one public class definition. The source code is converted to bytecode by the javac compiler. The javac compiler converts the .java file that you create to a .class file, which contains bytecode.

Syntax for compiling Java code Using javac:

Javac <filename.java>

Bytecode is independent of the platform that you use to execute Java programs. These files are interpreted by the interpreter, java.

The java Interpreter:

The java interpreter is used to execute complied Java applications. The bytecode that is the result of compilation is interpreted so that it can be executed.

Syntax for Executing a Java Application Using java:

Java <filename.class>

The appletviewer:

Applets are Java programs that are embedded in Web pages. You can run applets using a Web browser. The appletviewer let you run applets without the overhead of running a Web browser. You can test your applets using the appletviewer.

Syntax for executing a Java Applet:

Appletviewer<URL of the .html file>

The jdb Tool:

Debugging is the term used for identifying and fixing bugs(mistakes) in the program. These mistakes could be syntactical (Violation of a grammatical rule), logical or runtime (error due to an unexpected condition). You can use the Java debugging tool jdb to debug your Java program.

Syntax for Using jdb:

jdb<filename.class>

The javap Disassembler:

If you do not have the .java file but have the bytecode, you can retrieve the java code using a disassembler. The java disassembler, javap is used to recover the source code from the bytecode file.

Syntax for Using javap:

javap<list of .class files>

The filenames must be separated by spaces.

The Javadoc Tool:

The Javadoc is the document generator that create HTML page documentation for the classes that you create. To use Javadoc, you have to embed the statements between /** and */. The Javadoc tool has been used by Sun Microsystems for creating java documentation. This documentation is available at http://www.javasoft.com/doc.

Syntax for using Javadoc:

javadoc <list of .java files>

The filenames are separated by spaces.

The statements between /** and */ are called comment entries and are ignored by the compiler.

The javah Tool:

The javah tool creates header and stub files that let you extend your Java code with the C language.

Syntax for creating Header files:

javah<class filename>

The java compiler (javac) provides the keywords, syntax, data types and operators used in the java language. Their internal working is built into the compiler. Thus, when you write a command to add two integers, the compiler know how to achieve the result. The compiler also knows the error check that need to be carried out to ensure that the syntax is adhered to.

KEYWORDS:

Keywords are special words that are of significance to the java compiler. You cannot use keywords to name classes or variables. The table below contains a list of java keywords:

abstract	boolean	break	byte	case
catch	char	class	const	continue
default	do	double	else	extends
final	finally	float	for	goto
if	implements	import	instanceof	int
interface	long	native	new	package
private	protected	public	return	short
static	super	switch	synchronise	this
throw	throws	transient	try	void
volatile	while			

Data types:

The data that is stored in memory can be of many types. For example, a person's age is stored as a numeric value and an address is stored as alphanumeric characters. Data types are used to define the operations possible on them and the storage method.

The data types in java are classified as:

1) Primitive or standard data types.
2) Abstract or derived data types.

Primitive data types:

Primitive data types, also known as standards data types, are the data types that are built into the Java language. The Java compiler contains detailed instructions on each legal operation supported by the data type. There are eight primitive data types in Java.

Data type	Size/Format	Description	Range
Byte	8-bit	Byte-length integer	-128 to +127 if signed (-2^7 to 2^7-1) 0 to 255 if unsigned
Short	16-bit	Short integer	-32768 to +32767 (-2^{15} TO $2^{15}-1$)
int	32-bit	Integer	-2^{31} to $2^{31}-1$
long	64-bit	Long integer	-2^{63} to $2^{63}-1$
float	32-bit	Single-precision floating point	+/- about 10^{39}
double	64-bit	Double-precision floating point	+/- about 10^{317}
Other types			
char	16-bit	A single character	
boolean	1-bit	A boolean value (True or False)	

Note: - data is internally represented as binary digits (one and zeros). Bit stands for binary digit. A bit can store either 1 or 0.

Numerical data types:

Data type	Supports fractional values
byte	No
short	No
int	No
long	No
float	Yeas
double	No

All these data types can hold negative values. However, the keyword unsigned can be used to restrict the range of values to positive numbers. The data type boolean can hold only the values true or false and char can contain only a single character.

Java specifies the size and format of its primitive data types. The size and the format of the data types remain the same, no matter what platform (Operating system and network) you use.

Abstract or derived data types:

Abstract data types are based on primitive data types and have more functionality than primitive data types. For example, string is an abstract data type that can store letters, digits and other characters like / , () : ; $ and # .

You cannot perfume calculations on a variable of the string data type even if the data stored in it has digits. However, string provides methods for concatenating two strings, searching for one string within another, and extracting a portion of a string. The primitive data types do not have these features.

VARIABLES:

Java provides constants and variables for storing and manipulating data in programs.

Java allocates memory to each variable and constant that you use in your program. The values of variables may change in a program, but the values of constants, as the name suggests, do not change. You must assign unique names to variables and constants. Variable names are used in programs, in the same way as they are in algebra. Each variable that is used in a program must be declared.

Variable naming Conventions:

A program refers to a variable using its name. Certain rules and conventions govern the naming of variables. The rules are enforced by the programming language - your program will not compile if you have not followed the rules of the language.

Rules for naming variables:

- o The name of a variable needs to be meaningful, short and without any embedded space or symbol like - ? ! @ # % ^ & * ( ) [ ] { } . , ; : ' / and \
  However, underscores can be used wherever a space is required. For example, first_name.

- o Variable names must be unique. For example, to store four different numbers, four unique variable names.
- o A variable name must begin with a letter, a dollar symbol ('$') or an underscore ('_'), which may be followed by a sequence of letters or digits (0-9), '$' or '_'.
- o Keywords cannot be used for variable names. For example, you cannot declare a variable called switch (which is a keyword).

Variable naming conventions in Java:

- o Variable names must be meaningful. The names must reflect the data that the variables contain. For example, to store the age of a student, the variable name could be studentAge.
- o Variable names are nouns and begin with a lowercase letter.
- o Variable name contains two or more words, join the words and begin each word with an uppercase letter. The first word, however, starts with a lowercase letter. Examples of variable names:

    The following variable names are valid-

    addres1

    studentName

    thisVariableNameIsVeryLong

The following variable names are invalid-

#phone

1stName

Note: Java is case-sensitive. This means that studentAge is not the same as StudentAge. Following the naming conventions will help you to avoid such errors.

Variable Initialization:

You cannot use a variable without initializing it. When you create an object of a class, Java assigns default values to the primitive data type class variables. The following table displays the values that are used to initialise the data members of a class.

Data type	Initial Value
byte	0
short	0
int	0
long	0L
float	0.0
double	0.0
Char	\u000' (null)
boolean	false
abstract data type	null

For example, the integer x is automatically assigned the value 0 in the declaration given below:

int x;

The above values are assigned automatically only to the data members of a class that are of the primitive data types. You must initialise the variables that you declare in a method (local variables). The Java compiler returns an error if you do not initialize the variables that you have declared in a method.

Assigning values to variables:

Values can be assigned to variables in two ways:

> ➢ At the time of declaration.
> ➢ Anywhere in the program after the declaration and before use.

Syntax:

      <access_specifier><data_type><variable_name> =<value>;

Example:

      int salary=5000;

Syntax:

      <access_specifier><data_type><variable_name>;
      <variable_name> =<value>;

Example:

      int salary;
      salary=5000;

The symbol '=' is known as the assignment operator, and is used to assign values to variables.

Literals:

The variables in Java can be assigned constant values. The values assigned must match the data type of the variables. Literals are the values that may be assigned to primitive or string type variables and constants.

- o The Boolean literals are tree and false.
- o The integer literals are numeric data. They can be represented as octal (the number with a zero prefixed) or hexadecimal (the number prefixed with 0x).
- o floating-point literals are numbers that have a decimal fraction.
- o Character literals are enclosed in single quotes.
- o String literals are enclosed in double quotes.

You can assign a value to a variable or constant when you declare it (int marks=90;) or anywhere else in the program.

Syntax:<variable>=<value>;

Examples:

      x=true;   //Boolean literal
      x=1;   //integer literal
      x=2.3f;   //float literal
      x='a';   // character literal
      x=" string"; //string literal

Note: Every statement in the above lines of code ends with a semicolon (**;**). The semicolon is the *statement terminator* in Java.

OPERATORS:

Operators are used to compare values, and test multiple conditions. They can be classified as:

- o Arithmetic operators.
- o Assignment operators.
- o Unary operators.
- o Comparison operators.
- o Shift operators.
- o Bit-wise operators.
- o Logical operators.
- o Conditional operators.
- o The *new* operator.

Arithmetic Operators:

Operator	Description	Example	Explanation
+	Adds the operands.	x=y + z;	Adds the value of y and z and store the result in x.
-	Subtracts the right operand from the left operand.	x = y -z;	Subtracts z from y and stores the result in x.
*	Multiplies the operands.	x = y * z;	Multiplies the value y and z and store the result in x.
/	Divides the left operand by the right operand.	x= y / z;	Divides y by z and stores the result in x.
%	Calculates the remainder of an integer division.	x=y % z;	Divides y by z and stores the remainder in x.

Assignment Operators:

Operator	Description	Example	Explaination
=	Assigns the value of the right operand to the left.	X = y	Assigns the value of y to x.
+=	Adds the operands and assigns the result to the left operand.	x +=y	Adds the value of y to x. The expression cloud be written as x =x + y;
-+	Subtracts the right operand from the left operand and stores the result in the left operand.	X - = y	Subtracts y from x. Equivalent to x = x − y
*=	Multiplies the left operand by the right operand and stores the result in the left operand.	x *= y	Multiplies the values x and y and stores the result in x. Equivalent to x = x * y
/=	Divides the left operand by the right operand and stores the result in the left operand.	x /= y	Divides x by y and stores the result in x. Equivalent to x = x / y
%=	Divides the left operand by the right operand and stores the remainder in the left operand.	X %= y	Divides x by y and stores the remainder in x. Equivalent to x = x % y

Any of the operators used as shown below:

x<operator>=y

Can be represented as,x = x<operator> y

Unary Operators:

Operator	Description	Example	Explanation
++	Increase the value of the operand by one.	x++	Equivalents to x=x+1
--	Decrease the value of the operand by one.	x--	Equivalent to x=x-1

Prefix and postfix Notations:

- o As a prefix, in which the operator precedes the variable: ++Var;

- o As a postfix, in which the operator follows the variable: Var++;

Comparison Operators (Relational Operators) :

Comparison operators evaluate to true or false.

Operator	Description	Example	Explanation
= =	Evaluates whether the operands are equal.	x = = y	Returns true if the values are equal and false if otherwise.
!=	Evaluates whether the operands are not equal.	x! = y	Returns true if the values are not equal and false if otherwise.
>	Evaluates whether the left operand is greater than the right operand.	x > y	Returns true if x is greater than y and false if otherwise.
<	Evaluates whether the left operand is less than the right operand.	x < y	Returns true if x is less than y and false if otherwise.
>=	Evaluates whether the left operand is greater than or equal to the right operand.	x >= y	Returns true if x is greater than or equal to y and false if otherwise.
<=	Evaluates whether the left operand is less than or equal to the right operand.	x <= y	Returns true if x is less than or equal to y and false if otherwise.

Shift Operators:

Data is stored internally in binary format (in the form of bits). A bit can have a value of one or zero. Eight bits form a byte. Shift operators work on bits of data. Using the shift operator involves moving the bit pattern left or right. You can use them only on integer data types and not on char, boolean, float or double data type.

Operator	Description	Example	Explanation
>>	Shifts bits to the right, filling sign bits at the left and it is also called the signed right shift operator.	x = 10 >> 3	The result of this is 10 divided by 2^3. An explanation is given below.
<<	Shifts bit to the left filling zeros at the right.	x = 10 << 3	The result of this is 10 multiplied by 2^3. An explanation is given below.
>>>	Also called the unsigned shift operator, works like the >> operator, but fills in zeros from the left.	x = -10>>>3	An explanation is given below.

Shifting Positive Numbers:

The int data type occupies four bytes in the memory. The rightmost eight bits of the number 10 are represented in binary as

0	0	0	0	1	0	1	0

When you do a right shift by 3 (10 >> 3), the result is

0	**0**	**0**	0	0	0	0	1

$10/2^3$, which is equivalent to 1.

When you do a left shift by 3 (10<<3), the result is

0	1	0	1	0	**0**	**0**	**0**

$10*2^3$, which is equivalent to 80.

Bit-Wise Operators:

Operator	Description	Example	Explanation
& (AND)	Evaluates to a binary value after a bit wise AND on the two operands.	x & y	AND results in a 1 if both the bits are 1, any other combination results in a 0.
/ (OR)	Evaluates to a binary value after a bit wise OR on the two operands.	x / y	OR results in a 0 when both the bits are 0, any other combination results in a 1.
^ (XOR)	Evaluates to a binary value after a bit wise XOR on the two operands.	x ^ y	XOR results in a 0 if both the bits are of the same value and 1 if the bits have different values.
~ (inversion)	Converts all 1 bits to 0s and all 0 bits 1s.	~x	It returns the inverse or complement of the bit. It makes every 0 a 1 and every 1 a 0.

Logical Operators: Use logical operators to combine the results of Boolean expressions.

Operator	Description	Example	Explanation
&&	Evaluates to *true* if both the conditions evaluate to *true, false* if otherwise.	x>5 && y<10	The result is *true* if condition1 (x>5) and condition2 (y<10) are both *true*. If one of them is *false*, the result is *false*.
//	Evaluates to *true* if at least one of the conditions is evaluate to *true*, and *false* if none of the conditions evaluates to *true*.	x>5 // y<10	The result is *true* if either condition1 (x>5) or condition2 (y<10) or both evaluate to *true*. If both the conditions are*false*, the result is *false*.

Conditional Operators:

(condition)? val1: var2	Evaluates to val1 if the condition returns *true* and val2 if the condition returns *false*.	x = (y>z) ? y : z	x is assigned the value of y if y is greater than z, else x is assigned the value of z.

Syntax : The general syntax of ternary operator is as follows –

variable =(condition)? expressionTrue : expressionFalse;

Consider the following statements that find the maximum of two given numbers:

if (num1 > num2)

{

      Max = num1;

}

else

{

      Max = num2;

}

In the above program code, we are determining whether *num1* is greater than *num2*. The variable *Max* is assigned the value *num1* if the expression (num1>num2) evaluates to *true* and is assigned the value *num2* if the expression evaluates to*false*. The above program code can be modified using the conditional operator as:

      Max = (num1 > num2) ? num1 : num2;

The **? :** operator is called the ternary operator since it has three operands.

The new Operator:

When you create an instance of a class, you need to allocate memory for it. When you declare an object, you merely state its data type. For example,

Pen blackPen;

This tells the compiler that the variable *blackPen* is an object of the *Pen* class. It does not allocate memory for the object.

To allocate memory, you need to use the *new* operator.

Syntax:

You can allocate memory for an object in two ways:

1. Declare the object and then allocate memory using the *new* operator.
<class_name><object_name>;

<object_name> = new <class_name>();

2. Declare the object and at the same time allocate memory using the new operator.
<class_name><object_name> = new <class_name>( );

Example:

Method 1

Pen blackPen;
blackPen = new Pen();

Method 2

Pen blackPen = new Pen();

Note: You can use the new operator only inside methods.

ORDER OF PRECEDENCE OF OPERATORS:

The following table shows the order of precedence of operators. Those with the same precedence are listed in the same row. The order can be changed by using parentheses at appropriate places.

Type	Operators
High Precedence	[], ()
Unary	+, -, ~, !, ++, --
Multiplicative	*, /, %
Additive	+, -
Shift	<<, >>, >>>
Relational	<, <=, >=, >
Equality	==, !=
Bit-wise	&, ^, /
Logical	&&, //
Conditional	?:
Assignment	=, +=, -=, *=, %=

All the operator except the assignment operators is left-associative, that is, they operate from the left to the right.

Type Conversion (Casting):

Every expression has a type that is determined by the components of the expression. Consider the following statements:

> double x;
>
> int y =2;
>
> float z = 2.2f;
>
> x = y + z;

The expression to the right of the '=' operator is solved first. The resulting value is stored in x. The expression on the right has variables of two different numeric data types, *int* and *float*. The *int* value is automatically promoted to the higher data type *float* and then, the expression is evaluated. The resulting expression is of the *float* data type. This value is then assigned to x, which is a *double* (larger range than *float*), and therefore, the result is a *double*.

Java automatically promotes values to a higher data type, to prevent any loss of information.

Consider the following statement:

> int x = 5.5/2;

Consider the following statement:

> int x = 5.5/2;

The expression on the right evaluates to a decimal value and the expression on the left is an integer and hence, cannot hold a fraction. When you compile this code, the compiler will give you the following error.

"Incompatible type for declaration. Explicit cast needed to convert double to int."

This is because data can be lost when it is converted from a higher data type to a lower data type. The compiler requires that you typecast the assignment. To accomplish this, type the following:

> int x = (int) 5.5 / 2;

This is known as *Explicit Typecasting*. Explicit typecasting has to be done when there is a possibility of loss of data during conversion. The assignment between *short* and *char* also needs explicit typecasting.

Rules for typecasting
- A Boolean variable cannot be typecast.
- There is an implicit conversion for non-Boolean data if the conversion increases the range of data that can be stored.
- If the range is narrowed, an explicit typecasting is required.
- An implicit cast occurs in the following order:

> byte $\rightarrow$ short $\rightarrow$ int $\rightarrow$ long $\rightarrow$ float $\rightarrow$ double
>
> char $\rightarrow$ int $\rightarrow$ long $\rightarrow$ float $\rightarrow$ double

- Any other conversion needs to be typecast as it narrows the range of values that can be stored.

DECISION CONSTRUCTS:

We make decisions every day – which movie to watch, what ice cream to have, etc. Decision making is incorporated into programs as well. Its result determines the sequence in which a program will execute the instructions. You can control the flow of a program using decision constructs. They allow the selective execution of statements depending on the value of the expressions associated with them.

The if . . else Construct :

The if decision construct is followed by a logical expression in which data is compared and a decision is made based on the result of the comparison.

Syntax:

```
if (boolean_expr)

{

        statements;

}

else

{

        statements;

}
```

Example:

The following code finds the maximum of two numbers –

```
if ( num1 > num2)

{

      Max = num1;

}

else

{

      Max = num2;

}
```

The example determines which variable, *num1* or*num2*, holds a higher value. If the value of the variable *num1* is greater than that of *num2*, the statements in the *if* block are executed, otherwise the statements in the *else* block are executed. A block is defined as the set of statements between two curly braces   { }.

The switch Construct:

Another decision construct available in Java is the *switch...case*. It is used when there are multiple values for the same variable. The switch statement successively tests the value of an expression or a variable against a list of integer or character constants. When a match is found, the statements associated with *case* constant are executed.

Instead of writing many *if...else* statements, you can usethe switch statement.The switch statement selects one of many statements to be executed

Syntax:

```
switch(variable_name) {
        case expr1:
                statements;
                break;
        case expr2:
                statements;
                break;
        ...............
        Case expr n:
                statements;
                break;
        default:
                statements;
}
```

The keyword *switch* is followed by the variable in parentheses:

switch(x)

Each case keyword is followed by a *case* constant:

Case 1 :

The data type of the case constant should match that of the *switch* variable. Before entering the *switch* constant, a value should have been assigned to the *switch* variable.

The *default* keyword:

The example below uses the weekday number to calculate the weekday name:

```
int day = 4;
switch (day) {
        case 1:
```

```java
                System.out.println("Monday");

            break;

        case 2:

                System.out.println("Tuesday");

            break;

        case 3:

                System.out.println("Wednesday");

            break;

        case 4:

                System.out.println("Thursday");

            break;

        case 5:

                System.out.println("Friday");

            break;

        case 6:

                System.out.println("Saturday");

            break;

        case 7:

                System.out.println("Sunday");

            break;

    }
    // Outputs "Thursday" (day 4)
```

The *break* Keyword:

The *break* statement causes the program flow to exit from the body of the *switch* construct. Control goes to the first statement followed the end of the *switch* construct. If the *break* statement is not used, the control passes to the next *case* statement and the remaining statements in the *switch* construct are executed.

When Java reaches a break keyword, it breaks out of the switch block.This will stop the execution of more code and case testing inside the block.When a match is found, and the job is done, it's time for a break. There is no need for more testing.

A *break* can save a lot of execution time because it "ignores" the execution of all the rest of the code in the switch block.

The *default* Keyword:

The statements associated with the *default* keyword are executed if the value of the *switch* variable does not match any of the *case* constants. The *default* label, if used, must be the last option in the *switch* construct.

The default keyword specifies some code to run if there is no case match:

int day = 4;

switch (day) {

    case 6:

        System.out.println("Today is Saturday");

        break;

    case 7:

        System.out.println("Today is Sunday");

        break;

    default:

        System.out.println("Looking forward to the Weekend");

}

// Outputs "Looking forward to the Weekend"

Note: That if the *default* statement is used as the last statement in a switch block, it does not need a *break*.

LOOPING CONSTRUCTS:

A *loop* causes a section of a program to be repeated a certain number of times. The repetition continues while the condition set for it remains *true*. When the condition becomes *false*, the *loop* ends and the control is passed to the statement following the *loop*.

The *while* Loop:

The *while* loop is a looping construct available in Java. The *while* loop continues until the evaluating condition becomes *false*. The evaluating condition has to be a logical expression and must return a *true* or *false* value. The variable that is checked in the boolean expression is called the *loop control variable*.

Syntax:

while(boolean_expr)

    {

        statements;

    }

You can use the if construct, and the break and continue keywords within the while block to execute selective statements or to exit the loop.

Example:

The following code generates the Fibonacci series between 1 and 200. In this series, each number is the sum of its two preceding numbers. The series start with 1.

```
int num1 = 1, num2 = 1;

System.out.println(num1);

while(num2 < 200)

{
        System.out.println(num2);

        num2 +=num1;

        num1 = num2 – num1;

}
```

Output:

```
1
1
2
3
5
8
13
21
34
55
89
144
```

The *System.out.println* () method display the output on the screen. Ensure that the loop control variable is appropriately initialised before the *while* construct is entered.

The break statement:

The *break* statement causes the program flow to exit from the body of the *while* loop. The following program code illustrates the use of the *break* statement.

```
int num = 1, num = 1;

System.out.println(num1);

while (num1 < 150)

{
        System.out.println(num2);

        num2 +=num1;
```

```
        num1 = num2 – num1;
        if (num2 == 89)
                break;
    }
```

The output of the above program:

```
        1
        1
        2
        3
        5
        8
        13
        21
        34
        55
```

The control exits the loop when the condition num2 == 89 become true.

The *continue* statement:

The *continue* statement returns the control to the beginning of the *while* loop, skipping any statement following the *continue* statement in the loop body.

The *do ... while* Loop:

In a *while* loop, the condition is evaluated at the beginning of the loop. If the condition is *false*, the body of the loop is not executed. If the body of the loop must be executed at least once, then the do...*while* loop construct should be used. The *do...while* construct places the test expression at the end of the loop.

The keyword *do* marks the beginning of the loop. The braces delimit the body of the loop. Finally, a *while* statement provides the condition and end the body of the loop.

Syntax:

```
do
{
Statements;
}while(boolean_expr);
```

Example:

```
    num = 11;
    do
    {
            num++;
    } while( num< 10);
```

In the above *do..while* loop, the condition – *while*(num<10) – is evaluated only after the body of the loop has been executed once. Therefore, the value of *num* is increased by 1. If the same code were written in a *while* loop, the loop would not be executed.

The for Loop:

The *while* and *do...while* loos are used when the number of *iterations* (the number of times the loop body is executed) is not known. The *for* loop is used in situations when the number of iterations is known in advance. For example, it can be used to determine the square of each of the first ten numbers.

The *for* statement consists of the keyword *for*, followed by parentheses containing three expressions, each separated by a semicolon. These are the initialization expression, the test expression and the increment/decrement expression.

Syntax:

for(initialization_expr;test_expr;increment_expr/decrement_expr)

```
{
      Statement;
}
```

in the statement,for (var = 0; var < =10; var++)

var = 0 is the initialization expression. var <= 10 is the test expression, and var++ is the increment expression. Here, var is the loop variable. The body of the *for* loop is enclosed within braces.

Initialization: The initialization expression is executed only once, when the control is passed to the loop for the first time. It gives the loop variable an initial value.

Test expression: The condition is executed each time the control passes to the beginning of the loop. The body of the loop is executed only after the condition has been checked. If the condition evaluates to *true*, the loop is executed, otherwise, the control passes to the statement following the body of the loop.

Increment/Decrement expression: The increment/decrement expression is always executed when the control returns to the beginning of the loop.

Example:

```
//This code snippet calculates and print the square of the first ten natural numbers

int var;

for (var = 1; var <=10; var++)

{
        System.out.println(var * var);

}
```

The output of the program is : 1   4   9   16   25   36   49   64   81   100

Arrays:

Have you ever noticed the way hotel rooms are numbered in a linear manner? You find a row of rooms that have a continuous numbering pattern. Each room is organized by its number. If you were to send a bouquet of flowers to your friend who stays in room number 121 at Hotel Vivanta, you would probably write the address as:

Room number 121, Hotel Vivanta.

In fact, any room would be addressed in a similar way. There are two parts to the address specified above.

1. The hotel name.
2. The room number.

An *array* is a representation of data in contiguous spaces in the memory of your computer. All the variables of the *array* have the same name just as all the rooms at Hotel Vivanta. The room number in the hotel is the *index*(or subscript) of the variables (elements) in the *array*.

Each element in the *array* is distinguished by the *index*. All the elements in an array must be of the same data type. For example, you cannot have one element of the *int* data type and another of the *boolean* data type in the same array. An array is a collection of elements of the same type that are referenced by a common name. Each element of an array can be referred to by an array name and a subscript or index. To create and use an *array* in Java, you need to first declare the *array* and then initialize it. Single-dimensional and two-dimensional*arrays* are described below:

Single-dimensional array:

Syntax: To declare a single-dimensional array, the syntax is:

data type [ ] variablename;

Example:

int [ ] numbers;

The above statement will be declaring a variable that can hold an array of *float* type variables. After declaring the variable for the array, the array needs to be created in the memory. This can be done by using the new operator in the following way:

number = new int[10];

This statement assigns ten contiguous memory locations of the type *int* to the variable *numbers*. The *array* can store ten elements.

Initializing the array can be done using the *for* loop as given below:

```
for (int var=0; var < 10; var++)

{

        numbers[var]= var;

}
```

The *array* elements are stored in the memory are:

Value	Representation
0	numbers[0]
1	numbers[1]
2	numbers[2]
3	numbers[3]
4	numbers[4]
5	numbers[5]
6	numbers[6]
7	numbers[7]
8	numbers[8]
9	numbers[9]

Two-Dimensional Arrays:

A two-dimensional *array* can be thought of as a table of rows and columns.

Syntax:

The general syntax for declaring a two-dimensional *array* is:

Data type[ ] [ ] variablename;

Example-

int [ ] [ ] numbers;

To create the *array* in the memory, the following statement can be used:

numbers = new int[3][3];

This will create a two-dimensional *array* of nine elements – *three rows* and *three columns*. To initialize this *array*, multiple *for* loops can be used.

Example:

```
For (int varOuter = 0; varOuter< 3; varOuter++)

{

    For (int varInner = 0; varInner< 3; varInner)

        {

                numbers[varOuter][varInner] =0;

        }

}
```

This loop will ensure that all the elements of the array are initialized to zero.

Chapter 4:   Classes and Objects

Objectives:

- o   Declaring classes.
- o   Writing comment entries.
- o   Creating objects.
- o   Indenting programs.
- o   Declaring variables.
- o   Declaring methods.
- o   Passing arguments to methods.
- o   Constructors.
- o   Access specifiers.
- o   Modifiers.
- o   The *main ()* method.
- o   Overloading.

CLASSES:

Consider a company that has hundred of employees. It helps the management if the employees are organised into different departments, each having defined responsibilities. Each department would know how to handle the responsibilities assigned to it. For example, the Human Resources (HR) department would know how to recruit people and prepare paychecks. Employees of the other departments would only be interested in taking paychecks and not how they were created.

Similarly, classes help you to organize tasks and assign them to entities. You can encapsulate the data and restrict access to it. You can build hierarchies of classes. Classes help you to reuse data and code. When you instantiate a class, you create an object. Objects are the building blocks of object-oriented programming.

Declaring a Class:

A class defines the behaviour of an object. For example, a building is constructed based on an architectural blueprint. Many buildings can be constructed from the same blueprint, but each instance of a building will have its own state and set of attributes.

A class is just a mould that helps in creating an object and is not the object itself. You can create several instances(object) of a class. The general syntax for creating a class is as follows –

Syntax:

A class has data members(attributes) and behaviours (methods). The data members and methods of a class are defined inside a class body. In Java, braces ({ }) mark the beginning and end of a class or method. Braces are also used to delimit blocks of code in loops and iterative constructs. The generic syntax for creating a class in Java is:

[<access_specifier>] [<modifier>] class <class_name>

{

    //statements

}

Class Name:

A class name is mandatory and must be given while declaring a class. The class name is used to refer to the class and to create instances of the class.

The *class* keyword is used to declare a class.

The <access_specifier> and <modifier> are optional.

Example:

```
Class Camera

{

        //data members

        // methods

}
```

Comment Entries:

A double backslash '//' used in the above code marks the beginning of a *comment entry* (also called a comment). A comment is a message for a programmer and describes a class, a method, or even a statement. Java support three types of comments, which are-

1. Multiple-line comments- Anything you write between /* and */ is treated as a comment. The text that you type here can span many lines.
   ```
   /* multiple line
   Comments   */
   ```
2. Single-line comment – Anything you type after // is treated as a comment. The text cannot span more than a line. If you have multiple lines as comments, you must start every line with //.
   ```
   // single line comment.
   ```
3. The *javadoc* comment – These comments are used by the javadoc utility to create documentation. These comments are similar to the multiple-line comments but start with a /** instead of */.

   ```
   /** This is a
    javadoc comment  **/
   ```

Naming Classes:

Rules for Naming Classes : A class name-

- o   Must not be a keyword in Java.
- o   Can begi with a letter, an underscore '_' or a '$' symbol.
- o   Must not contain embedded spaces or periods.
- o   Can contain characters from various alphabets, like Japanese, and Hebrew.
  Conventions for naming Classes:
- o   A class name must be meaningful. It usually represents a real life class. For example, Camera.
- o   Class name are nouns and begin with an uppercase letter.

Creating an Object:

An object is an instance of a class. Declaring an object is similar to declaring a variable.

Syntax:

                    <class_name><object>;

Example

      Camera kodak36;

You must allocate memory to object before you use them. This is done using the *new* operator.

      Kodak36 = new Camera();

DATA MEMBERS:

If you were to describe a camera, you would list its physical attributes like the model, the shutter speed, and the price. You would also list the functionality it provides (auto rewind, auto focus, and click). All data members and methods are declared within the class body.

Declaring Data Members:

      Syntax:

            The syntax for declaring a data member is:

      [<access_specifier>] [<modifier>] <data_type><variable_name>;

The [<access_specifier> and <modifier> are optional. The declaration is terminated with a semicolon. The <data_type> can be any valid Java data type, depending upon the kind of data to be stored.

The <variable_name> is mandatory while declaring a variable. The name of a variable is subsequently used to refer to that variable.

Example:

      Class Cemera

      {

            float price;

            string modelName;

      }

Indentation:

      If you notice, in the above code, the declaration of the data members has been shifted to the right. This is known as *indentation*. Indentation is an industry standard that aims at making code legible. You can indent code using the Tab key or use the Spacebar to key in the required number of spaces.

Naming Variables:

Rules for naming Variables: A variable name -

o   Must not be a keyword in Java.
o   Must not begin with a digit.
o   Can begin with a letter, an underscore '_' or a '$' symbol.
o   Must not contain embedded spaces.
o   Can contain characters from various alphabets, like Japanese, Greek, Cyrillic, and Hebrew.

Conventional for Naming Variables:
o   Variable name must be meaningful. The names must reflect the data the variables contain. For example, to store the age of a student, the variable name could be studentAge.
o   Variable names are nouns and begin with a lowercase letter.
o   If a variable name contains two or more words, join the words and begin each word with an uppercase letter. The first word, however, starts with a lowercase letter.

Example : The following variable names are valid-

number

stud_Age

dateOfJoin

The following variable names are invalid:
#number
Emp.age
Date of join

METHODS:

A television is a class that has attributes (colour, dimensions, and speakers) and methods (brightness, contrast, volume, switch on/off, and select). The volume method raises or lowers the volume whereas the select method allows you to select a channel of your choice and returns the channel number. Imagine a television that does not have a volume method!

Looking at the analogy above, it is clear that methods are essential to a class.

Declaring Methods:

Syntax:

[<access_specifier>] [<modifier>] <return_type><method_name> ([argument_list])

```
{

        // statements

}
```

<return_type>:

The return type of a method is the data type of the value that is returned by the method.

For example,

Void displayStdName( ) – Return no value, therefore the return type of the method is void.

float calculateAllowance( ) – Returns a value of the *float* data type. Therefore, the return type of the method is float.

<method_name>: A method name must follow naming conventions. Since methods are also the behaviour of a class, a method name should be a verb-noun combination. After defining a method, you can use its name to execute the method.

For example:-

displayStdName();

<argument_list>: An argument list is the set of information that is passed to a method. It is specified within parentheses.

For Example,

booleanapplyLeave (int days);

The following code shows the declaration of methods in a class.

Class Camera

{

    void clickButton ()

    {

        // This method does not take any arguments and does not return any value.

    }

    int countPhotographs ()

    {

        // This method does not take any arguments and returns the number of
        //photographs taken – an integer

    }

    booleanchangeShutterSpeed(int numberOfMiliSecond)

    {

        // This method takes a parameter of the int data type and returns a boolean
        //variable (true if the action was successful and false otherwise).

    }

Naming Methods:

Rules for Naming Methods: A method name-

- o Must not be a key word in Java.
- o Must not begin with a digit.

o Can begin with a letter, an underscore '_' or a '$' symbol.
o Must not contain embedded spaces or periods '.' .
o Can contain characters from various alphabets, like Japanese, Greek, Cyrillic, and Hebrew.

USING CLASS MEMBERS:

Using data Members: Once the data members are declared, you can initialize and use them for calculations and other operations, using a data member from the same class.

Example:
Class Camera
{

    float price;
    string modelName;
    int noOfPhotos;

    void increamentNoOfPhotos ()

    {

    // This method increaments the number of photographs taken noOfPhotos++;

    }

}

Using a Data Member from Another Class

A data member can be used in a different class by creating an object of that class and then referring to that method using the dot '.' operator.

You can create an object of a class by using the new operator.

Example:

Class Robot
{
    // declaring an object of the Camera class.
    Camera eyes;
    void takePhotograph ()
    {
        //allocating memory to the object
        eyes = *new*Camera();
    // incrementing the number of photograph taken
        eyes.noOfPhotos++;
    }
}

Invoking a Method:
To invoke a method, the method name must be followed by parentheses and a semicolon. One method of a class can be invoke another method of the same class using the name of the method.

Example:

```
Class Camera
{
        float price;
        string modelName;
        int noOfPhotos;
        void clickButton ()
        {
                // calling the increamentNoOfPhotos from the same class
                increamentNoOfPhotos();

        }
        void incrementNoOfPhotos()
        {
                // This method increaments the number of photographs taken.
        }


}
```

Passing Arguments to a Method:

You can code methods that accept arguments and accomplish the assigned task based on those arguments. Take an example of a library. One of the methods of a *librarian* class is *issueBook()*. The librarian cannot issue a bookuntil you specify the book you want. Therefore, the *issueBook()*method of the *librarian* class must take an argument, that is, the name of the book you want.

Example:

```
Class Librarian
{
        void callIssueBook()
        {
                String passName;
                passName = new String("Python Programming");
                //passing an argument to issueBook()
                issueBook(passName);
        }
        void issueBook(String recName)        //method with an argument
        {
                System.out.println("The name of the book is " +  recname);
        }
}
```

In the code given above, the *callIssueBook()* method calls the method *issueBook()*. Therefore, the method *callIssueBook()* is the calling method and *issueBook()* is the called method.

Two ways of passing arguments to a method are: -

- o Call by value.
- o Call by reference.

Call by value:

In Java, all arguments of the primitive data type are *passed by value*, which means that the original value of the argument cannot be altered by the *called* method. The *called* method gets only a copy of the variable. This means that any change made to the object by the *called* method is not reflected in the *calling* method. The following diagram explains this.

```
Calling ( )                                 passIt
   {
        Int passIt = 90;                      ┌──────┐
        Called(passIt);                       │  90  │
        System.out.println(passIt);           └──────┘
   }
                                                         New
                                                         Memory
   Called(int receiveIt)                                 Address
   {                                          ceiveIt
        receiveIt = 0;                        ┌──────┐
   }                                          │  90  │
                                              └──────┘
```

Call by Value

In a call by value, a copy of the argument's value is passed to the *called()* method which is maintained at a separate memory location. Therefore, when the *called()* method changes the value of the argument, the change is not reflected in the *calling()* method.

The output of the above snippet is 90.

Call by Reference:

Arguments that are objects, are *passed by reference* to the called method. This means that any change made to the object by the *called* method is reflected in the *calling* method.

In a call by reference, the memory address (reference) of the argument's variable is passed to the *called* method. Therefore, when the *called()* method changes the value of the argument, the change is reflected in the *calling()* method.

```
Calling ( )
   {
        Person passIt = new Person();
        passIt.name = "Kapil";
        called(passIt);
        System.out.println(passIt.name);
   }
```

```
Called(Person receiveIt)
{
        receiveIt.name = "Changed";

}
```

The output of the above snippet is "Changed".

CONSTRUCTORS:

The concept of object-orientation is drawn from real life. You need to initialize the value of certain data members when you create an object. You could write a method, say *initializeData()* in a class and call this method after creating the object. You could write the code for initializing the variables in the method *initializeData()*. But, how will you ensure that everybody who uses the class uses the method?

Java solves the problem by providing you a special method – the *constructor*. A *constructor* contains the code for initializing the data members of a class. It is executed automatically when an object of the class is created. Therefore, no matter who creates an object of the class, the *constructor* is invoked and the data members are initialized.

The constructor has the same name as that of the class in which it is defined.

Example:

```
Class Cake
{
        String message;
        double weight;
        String shape;

        Cake ()
        {
                message = "Happy Birthday, Mom";
                weight = 2;
                shape = "Square";
        }
}
```

In the above example, whenever an object of the *Cake* class is created, the *constructor* is executed and it initializes the member variables to the specified values.

Rules for Constructors:
  o A constructor has the same name as that of the class for which it is declared since it is called automatically when an object is created.
  o A constructor does not have a return type. A you do not call the constructor explicitly, you cannot use the return value anyway.

ACCESS SPECIFIERS:

An access specifier determines which features of a class (the class itself, the data members, and the methods) may be used by other classes. Java supports three access specifiers (also known as access modifiers).

- The *public* access specifier.
- The *private* access specifier.
- The *protected* access specifier.

The public Access Specifier:

All classes except *inner classes* (classes within other classes) can have the *public* access specifier. You can use a *public* class, a data member, or a method from any object in any Java program.

Example:

```
public class PublicCalss
{
        public int publicVariable;
        public void publicMethod();
        {
                ……………..
        }
}
```

The private Access Specifier:

Only objects of the same class can access a *private* variable or method. You can declare only variables, methods, and inner classes as *private*.

The protected Access Specifier:

Variables, methods, and inner classes that are declared *protected* are accessible to the subclasses of the class in which they are declared.

Default Access:

If you do not specify any of the above access specifiers, the scope is *friendly*. A class, variable, or method that has friendly. A class, variable, or method that has friendly access is accessible to all the classes of a package. (A package is a collection of classes).

In Java, *friendly* is not a keyword. It is a term that is used for the access level when no access specifier has been specified. You cannot declare a class, variable, or method with the friendly specifier.

MODIFIERS:

Modifiers determine how the data members and methods are used in other classes and object.

The static Modifier:

Consider a class, *Student*. You have created many objects of the *Student* class, and want to know how many objects you have created. How would you do that?

What you need here is a variable (counter) that is maintained by the class itself and not by the individual objects. Every time an object of the class is created, the constructor should increment the counter. Thus, the value of the counter would indicate the number of objects created.

The *static* modifier allows a variable or method to be associated with its class. A class cannot be declared *static*. Static variables are shared by all the instances of a class. You can access a *static* variable or method using the class name as shown below,

> ExampleClass.staticvariable;
> ExampleClass.staticMethod();

You need not create an object of the *class* to call a *static* method or variable. The variables and methods declared using the *static* keyword are called *class variables* and *class methods*.

The Final Modifier:

The *final* keyword is used for security reasons. Consider a situation where you do not want your class to be subclassed, or the value of a data member to be changed. The *final* modifier does not allow the class to be inherited. It is used to create classes that serve as a standard, and you do not want anybody to override the methods and use them in a different manner.

The final modifier implements the following restrictions:

- A *final* class cannot be inherited.
- A *final* method cannot be changed (override) by a subclass.
- A *final* data member cannot be changed after initialization.
- All methods and data members in a final class are implicitly *final*.

You can define constants using the *final* keyword. The compiler forces you to initialize *final* variables in the declaration statement itself.

Abstract Classes:

Abstract classes allow the implementation of a behaviour in different ways. The classes and methods declared using the abstract modifier are incomplete. They are deliberately left incomplete. The implementation is done in subclasses. Only abstract classes can have abstract methods.

Restrictions:

- An *abstract* class cannot be instantiated because the class is incomplete.
- Subclasses must override the *abstract* methods of the super class.

The Java compiler forces you to declare a class as abstract when:

- A class has one or more abstract methods.
- A class inherits an abstract method and does not override it.

The Native Modifier:

A *native* modifier can be used only for methods. It is used to tell the compiler that the method has been coded in a non-Java language such as C or C++. *Native* methods are platform-dependent. The body of a *native* method lies outside the Java environment. Therefore, writing native methods must be avoided. They are used when you have an existing code in another language and do not want to rewrite the code in Java.

The transient Modifier:

Object can be written to files and thus, saved for further use. You can use the *transient* modifier if you do not want to store a certain data member to a file. The *transient* modifier is used only with data members. *Transient* variables cannot be final or static.

The synchronized Modifier:

The *synchronized* modifier is used in multithreaded programs. A thread is a unit of execution within' a process. In a multithreaded program, you need to *synchronize* various threads.

Note: Access specifier determine the accessibility of data members from the objects of other classes. For example, a data member that is declared *private* cannot be accessed from an object of any other class.

Modifiers determine how data members are used in another objects. For example, a data member that has been declared as *static* can be accessed without the creation of an object of the class to which the data member belongs.

SCOPE OF VARIABLES:

Variables can be defined within a class, a method or a block. A block is defined as a set of statements between two curly braces – { } .

Local Scope:

Variables that are declared in a method or a block are called *local* variables as they are not accessible outside the method or block in which they are declared. They are also referred to as *automatic* (or auto) variables. Local variables are created and initialized every time the method is invoked or the program control enters the block. The variables are destroyed when the method or the block completes execution. Parameters of a method are also local to the method.

Class Scope:

The variable declared outside methods have a *class scope*. The variable and its value are retained as long as an object of the particular class exists, and can be used in all the methods of the class. If the variable is declared *public*, then the variable can be accessed from the objects of all classes.

The main() METHOD:

In Java application, you may have many classes, each class having many methods. The method that the compiler executes first is the *main()* method.

Rules for coding the main( ) method :

o   The syntax for main( ) is:

```
public static void main(String args[])
{
        ...........
}
```

The method is declared *public* so that the Java interpreter can access it. The method does not return a value and hence, has been declared *void*. The *static* modifier is used so that an instance of the class need not be created to call the *main( )* method.

o   The primary name of the file in which the code is written and the name of the class that has the *main( )* method should be the same.

For example, if you declare the *main*() method in the *TestMain* class, the name of the file must be *TestMain.java*.

If you try to execute a Java application that does not have a main( ) method, the following error message is printed:

Exception in thread "main" Java.lang.NoSuchMethodError: main

Example:

```
Class Camera
{
    public static void main(String args[])
    {
        if(args.length == 0)
        {
            System.out.println("Error: File name not entered");
            System.exit(0);
        }
.....//code for deleting the file is to be written here

        System.out.println("File deleted");
    }
}
```

The above code first validates whether the file name is passed from the command line. If the parameter is not passed, it prints an error message and exit. If the parameter is passed, it executes the rest of the statements.

Output:
The output of the program is shown below:
File deleted
The output of the program when the command line argument is not specified is:
Error: File name not entered.

OVERLOADING:

Method Overloading: There are times when you would want to create several methods that perform closely related tasks. For example, the class *Calculator* has a method that adds two integers, another method that adds two float values and a third method that adds a float and an integer value. These methods perform the same essential operation, and so, it is appropriate to use the same name for them. In programming languages that do not support overloading, you have to think of three different names for the methods that essentially do the same task.

Java supports method overloading and hence, the methods can be declared as follows:
- o   public void add(int a, int b);   //adds two integers
- o   public void add(float a, float b);   //adds two floats
- o   public void add(float a, int b);   //adds afloat and an integer

Example:

```
class Calculator
{
    public int add(int a, int b)
    {
        System.out.println("int  and int");
        return a + b;

    }
    public float add(float a, float b)
    {
        System.out.println("float  and float");
        return a + b;

    }
    public float add(float a, int b)
    {
        System.out.println("float  and int");
        return a + b;

    }
    public static void main(String args[])
    {
        Calculator c=new Calculator();
        System.out.println(c.add(1,10));
        System.out.println(c.add(1.6f,10.5f));
    }

}
```

In the above example, there are three add( ) methods. At the time of compilation, the compiler resolves the version of the add( ) method to be called based on the parameters passed.

Function Signature:

The signature of a method consists of:

o   The name of the method.
o   The number of arguments it takes.
o   The data type of the arguments.
o   The order of the arguments.

When you call a method, the compiler uses the signature of the method to resolve the method to be invoked. A class cannot have two methods having the same signature. This is because the compiler will not know which method to invoke if more than one method has the same signature. In the Calculator class, the methods have the same name but different parameters, and therefore, the signatures of the methods are different.

The return type of the method is not a part of its signature.

Chapter 4.1 : Relationship between Classes
Objectives:

In this section, you will learn about:
- ✓ Types of relationships.
- ✓ Superclasses and subclasses.
- ✓ Single and multiple inheritance.
- ✓ Implementing inheritance in Java.
- ✓ Interfaces.
- ✓ Overriding methods.

RELATIONSHIPS:

The procedural approach emphasizes actions that manipulate data. It does not clearly define relationships. In the object-oriented approach, objects perform actions in response to messages from other objects. This approach specifies relationships among classes depending on the behaviour of those classes.

Relationships are classified as follows:
- o A kind-Of relationship.
- o An Is-A relationship.
- o A Part-Of relationship.
- o A Has-A relationship.

Consider for a moment the similarities and differences among the following objects/classes: Automobile, Ford, Porsche, Truck, Car, and Engine We can make the following observations:
- ➢ A truck is a kind of an Automobile.
- ➢ A car is a (different) kind of an automobile.
- ➢ An engine is a part of an automobile.
- ➢ An automobile has an engine.
- ➢ The Ford is a car.

A Kind-Of Relationship:

Take the example of a human being and an elephant. Both are *'kind-Of'* mammals. Mammals have attributes – eye and limbs. They also have behaviour, for example, walk. As human beings and elephants are 'kind-Of' mammals, they share the attributes and behaviours of mammals. Human beings and elephants are subsets of the mammal class. The following figure depicts the relationship between the classes *Mammal* and *Humanbeing*.

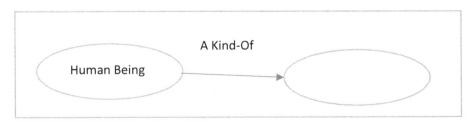

An Is-A Relationship:

The previous example depicts the relationship between human being and mammals. Let's take the instance of a human being, Joy, who 'is-a' human being and therefore, a mammal. The following figure depicts the 'is-a' relationship.

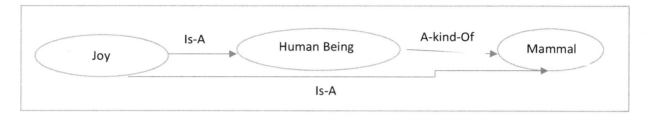

A Has-A Relationship/Part-Of Relationship:

A human being has a heart. This represents a '*has-a*' relationship. The same relationship can be represented as – the heart is a 'part-Of' a human being. The following figure depicts the relationship between a human being and the heart.

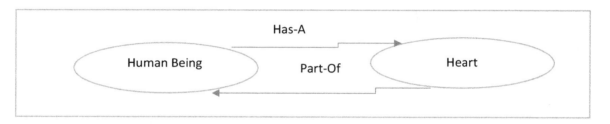

INHERITANCE:

Inheritance means that a class derives a set of attributes and related behaviour from a parent class. The philosophy behind inheritance is to portray things as they exist in the real world. For instance, a child inherits properties from both its parents.

Inheritance in Java is a mechanism in which one object acquires all the properties and behaviours of a parent object. It is an important part of OOPs (Object Oriented programming system).

Inheritance represents the IS-A relationship which is also known as a parent-child relationship.

Why use inheritance in java

- o For Method Overriding (so runtime polymorphism can be achieved).
- o For Code Reusability.

Terms used in Inheritance

Class: A class is a group of objects which have common properties. It is a template or blueprint from which objects are created.

Sub Class/Child Class: Subclass is a class which inherits the other class. It is also called a derived class, extended class, or child class.

Super Class/Parent Class: Superclass is the class from where a subclass inherits the features. It is also called a base class or a parent class.

Reusability: As the name specifies, reusability is a mechanism which facilitates you to reuse the fields and methods of the existing class when you create a new class. You can use the same fields and methods already defined in the previous class.

These all concepts terminologies are the basics in types of inheritance in Java.

Syntax: The general syntax is as follows-

class derived_class extends base_class

{

//methods

//fields

}

General Format :-

class superclass

{

// superclass data variables

// superclass member functions

}

class subclass extends superclass

{

// subclass data variables

// subclass member functions

}

For your kind information inheritance uses the "extends" keywords to produce derived classes while using the Base class. Extending keywords indicates the class to another class.

Extends Keyword:

The *extended* keyword is the indicator of a class to another class, like receiving the legacy from our forefathers by genetic inheritance of enzymes. It means class B inherits the attributes and methods from class A. It means now class A is a superclass and class B is playing the role of a subclass.

For example, in program:

class Base

{

public void M1()

{

System.out.println("Base Class Method");

```
}

}

class Derived extends Base

{

public void M2()

{

System.out.printIn(" Derived Class Methods ");

}

}

class Test

{

public static void main(String[] args)

{

Derived d = new Derived(); // creating object

d.M1(); // print Base Class Method

d.M2(); // print Derived Class Method

}

}
```

OUTPUT:

Base class method

Derived class method

Points to Remember

- ✓ Constructor cannot be inherited in Java.
- ✓ Private members do not get inherited in Java.
- ✓ Cyclic inheritance is not permitted in Java.
- ✓ Assign parent reference to child objects.
- ✓ Constructors get executed because of super() present in the constructor.

Types of Inheritance

- o Java supports the following four types of inheritance:
- o Single Inheritance
- o Multi-level Inheritance
- o Hierarchical Inheritance
- o Hybrid Inheritance

Single Inheritance

In single inheritance, a sub-class is derived from only one super class. It inherits the properties and behaviour of a single-parent class. Sometimes it is also known as simple inheritance.

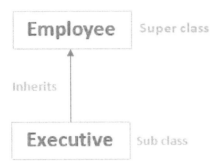

Single Inheritance

In the above figure, Employee is a parent class and Executive is a child class. The Executive class inherits all the properties of the Employee class.

Coding example of single inheritance:

```
class A
{
    int a, b;
    void display()
    {
        System.out.println("Inside class A values ="+a+" "+b);
    }
}
class B extends A
{
    int c;
    void show()
    {
    System.out.println("Inside Class B values="+a+" "+b+" "+c);
    }
}
class SingleInheritance
{
```

```
public static void main(String args[])
{
        B obj = new B( ); //derived class object
    obj.a=10;
    obj.b=20;
    obj.c=30;
    obj.display();
        obj.show();
    }
}
```

OUTPUT:

Inside class A values = 10 20

Inside class B values = 10 20 30

Multi-level Inheritance:

In multi-level inheritance, a class is derived from a class which is also derived from another class is called multi-level inheritance. In simple words, we can say that a class that has more than one parent class is called multi-level inheritance. Note that the classes must be at different levels. Hence, there exists a single base class and single derived class but multiple intermediate base classes.

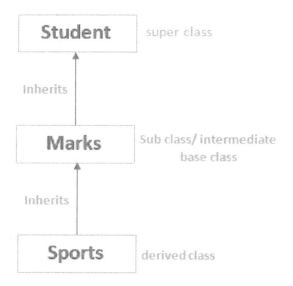

Multi-level Inheritance

In the above figure, the class Marks inherits the members or methods of the class *Students*. The class *Sports* inherits the members of the class *Marks*. Therefore, the *Student* class is the parent class of the class *Marks* and the class Marks is the parent of the class *Sports*. Hence, the class *Sports* implicitly inherits the properties of the *Student* along with the class Marks.

Hierarchical Inheritance:

If a number of classes are derived from a single base class, it is called hierarchical inheritance.

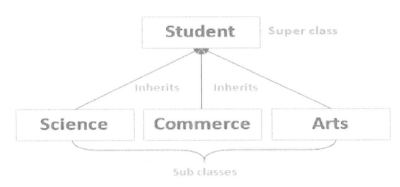

Hierarchical Inheritance

In the above figure, the classes *Science*, *Commerce*, and *Arts* inherit a single parent class named *Student*.

Hybrid Inheritance:

Hybrid means consist of more than one. Hybrid inheritance is the combination of two or more types of inheritance.

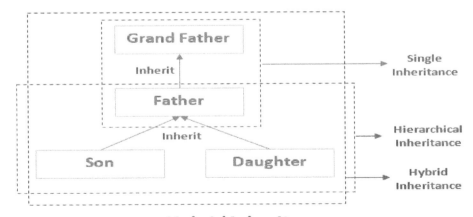

Hybrid Inheritance

In the above figure, *GrandFather* is a super class. The *Father* class inherits the properties of the *GrandFather* class. Since *Father* and *GrandFather* represents single inheritance. Further, the *Father* class is inherited by the *Son* and *Daughter* class. Thus, the *Father* becomes the parent class for *Son* and *Daughter*. These classes represent the *hierarchical inheritance*. Combinedly, it denotes the *hybrid inheritance*.

Chapter 5: Exception-Handling

Objectives:

In this section, you will learn about:

- ✓ The need for exception-handling.
- ✓ Exception classes.
- ✓ Exception-handling techniques.
- ✓ The try block
- ✓ The catch blocks.
- ✓ The throw statement.
- ✓ The throws statement.
- ✓ The finally statement.
- ✓ Use-defined exceptions.
- ✓ Common Exception.

EXCEPTIONS

The term *exception* denotes an *exceptional event*. It can be defined as an abnormal event that occurs during program execution and disrupts the normal flow of instructions.

Error-handling becomes a necessity when you develop applications that need to take care of unexpected situations. The unexpected situations that may occur during program execution are:

- o Running out of memory.
- o Resource allocation errors.
- o Inability to find files.
- o Problems in network connectivity.

Need for Exception-Handling:

You cannot afford to have an application that stops working or crashes if the requested file is not present on the disk. Traditionally, programmers used the return values of methods to detect errors that occurred at runtime. A variable *errno* was used for a numeric representation of the error. When multiple errors occurred in a methos, *errno* would have only one value- the value of the last error that occurred in the method.

Java handles exceptions the object-oriented way. You can use a hierarchy of exception classes to manage runtime errors. An exception provides a notifying programmers about an error.

The Exception Classes:

The class at the top of the hierarchy is called *Throwable*. Two classes are derived from the *Throwable* class – *Error* and *Exception*. The *Exception* class is used for the exceptional conditions that have to be trapped in a program. The *Error* class defines the conditions that do not occur under normal circumstances. In other words, the *Error* class is used for catastrophic failures such as *VirtualMachineError*. These classes are available in the *java.lang* package.

EXCEPTION-HANDLING TECHNIQUES:

When an unexpected error occurs in a method, Java creates an object of the type *Exception*. After creating the *Exception* object, Java sends it to the program, by an action called *throwing an exception*. The *Exception* object contains information about the type of error and the state of the program when the exception occurred. You need to handle the exception using an *exception-handler* and process the exception.

You can implement *exception-handling* in your program by using the following keywords:

- o *try*
- o *catch*
- o *throw*
- o *throws*
- o *finally*

Example:

Here is a sample code in which an exception is thrown:

```
public void myMethod (int num1, int num2)
{
        int result;
        result = num2/ num1;
        System.out.println("Result : " + result);
}
```

Output:

In the above piece of code an exception *java.lang.ArithmeticException* is thrown when the value of num1 is equal to zero. The error message displayed as:

Exception in thread "main" *java.lang.ArithmeticEception*: / by zero at \<classname\>.main(\<filename\>.java:8)

In the example, the Java environment tries to execute a division by zero, which result in a runtime error. An exception object is created to cause the program to stop and handle the exception. It expects an exception-handler to handle the exception raised. As the program has not been guarded for exceptions, the default exception-handler is invoked. The default exception-handler display the above message and terminates the program.

If you do not want the program to terminate, you have to trap the exception using *try* block.

The *try* Block:

You need to guard the statements that may throw an exception, in the try block.

Syntax:

```
try
{
        // statements that may cause an exception
}
```

The *try* block governs the statements that are enclosed within it and defines the scope of the exception-handlers associated with it. In other words, if an exception occurs within the *try* block, the appropriate exception-handler that is associates with the *try* block handles the exception. A *try* block must have at least one *catch* block that follows it immediately.

Example:

```
public void myMethod(int num1, int num2)
{
        int result;
        try
        {
                Result = num2 / num1;
        }
        catch(ArithmeticException e)
        {
                // Statements to handle exceptions
        }
        System.out.println("Result : " + result);
}
```

The catch Block:

You associate an exception-handler with the *try* block by providing one or more catch-handlers immediately after the *try* block.

Syntax:

```
try
{
        // statements that may cause an exception
}
catch(......)
{
```

```
        //error handling routines
}
```

The *catch* statement takes the object of the exception class that refers to the exception caught, as a parameter. Once the exception is caught, the statements within the *catch* block are executed. The scope of the *catch* block is restricted to the statements in the preceding *try* block only. The following code illustrate the use of the *catch* block.

Example:

```
public void myMethod(int num1, int num2)
{
        int result;
        try
        {
                result = num2 / num2;
        }
        catch(ArithmeticException e)
        {
                System.out.println("Error.... Divided by zero");
        }
        System.out.println("Result :" + result);
}
```

The compiler does not allow any statement between a *try* block and its associated *catch* blocks.

Mechanism of Exception-Handling:

In Java, the exception-handling facility handles abnormal and unexpected situations in a structured manner. When an exception occurs, the Java runtime system searches for an exception-handler (*try-catch* block) in the method that caused the exception. If a handler is not found in the current method, the handler is searched for in the calling method (the method that called the current method). The search goes on till the runtime system finds an appropriate exception-handler, that is, when the type of exception caught by the handler is the same as the type of the exception thrown.

Example:

```
        //DerivedClass.java
class BaseClass
{
        public int divide(int num1, int mun2)
        {
```

```
                return num1 /mun2;
            }
    }
    public class DerivedClass extends BaseClass
    {
            public int divide(int a, int b)
            {
                    return super.divide(a,b);
            }
            public static avoid main(String args[])
            {
                    int result =0;
                    DerivedClass d1 = new DerivedClass();
                    try
                    {
                            Result = d1.divide(100,0);
                    }
                    catch(ArithmeticException e)
                    {
                            Sysyem.out.println("Error  …. Division by Zero");
                    }
                      System.out.println("The result is : " + result);
            }

    }
```

Output:

Error …. Division by Zero

The result is : 0

In the above code, the*main*() method invokes the overridden method, divide( ), of the derived class. The derived class method, in turn, calls the divide( ) methodof the class with the parameters it *receives*. An exception occurs in the base class method. The Java runtime system looks for an exception-handler in the base class method first (the called method). Then, it looks for an exception-handler in the method of the derived class (the calling method). When it does not find the handler there, it shifts to the *main( )* method and executes the statements in the *catch* block of the method.

Multiple catch Blocks:

A single *try* block can have many *catch* blocks. This is necessary when the *try* block has statements that may raise different types of exceptions. The following code trapes three types of exceptions.

Example:

```
public class TryCatch

{

    public static void main(String args[ ] )
```

```
    {
            int array[ ] = {0,0};
            int num1, num2, result = 0;
            num1 = 100;
            num2 = 0;
            try
            {
                    result = num1/num2;
                    System.out.println 9num1 / array[2]);
                    //more statements
            }
            catch(ArithmeticException e)
            {
                    System.out.println("Error .......Division by Zero");
            }
            catch(ArrayIndexOutOfBoundsException e)
            {
                    System.out.println("Error .......out of Bound");
            }
            catch(Exception e)
            {
                    System.out.println("Some other Error");
            }
            System.out.println("The result is : " + result");
            //program proceeds
    }
}
```

In the code give above, the *try* block has many statements and each of the statements can result in an exception. Three *catch* blocks follow the try block, one for handling each type of exception. The *catch* block that has the most specific exception class must be written first.

Nested try and catch blocks

Nested *try* blocks are similar to nested constructs. You can have one *try-catch* block inside another. Similarly, a *catch* block can contain *try-catch* blocks. If a lower level *try-catch* block does not have a matching *catch* handler, the outer *try* block is checked for it.

The throw Statement:

You many want to throw an exception when a user enters a wrong login ID or password. You can use the *throw* statement to do so. The *throw* statement takes a single argument, which is an object of the *Exception* class.

Syntax:
            throw ThrowableInstance;

Example
            throw ThrowObject;
The compiler gives an error if the object *ThrowObject* does not belong to a valid Exception class. The *throw* statement is commonly used in programmer-defined exception.

The *throws* Statement

If a method is capable of raising an exception that it does not handle, it must specify that the exception has to be handled by the calling method. This is done using the *throws* statement. The *throws* statement is used to specify the list of exceptions that are thrown by the method.

Syntax:

[<access_specifier>][<modifier>]<return_type><method_name>(<arg_list>) [throws<exception_list>]

Example

```
    public void acceptPassword() throws IllegalAccessException
    {
            System.out.println("Intruder");
            Throw new IllegalAccessExpection;
    }
```

The finally Block :

When an exception is raised, the rest of the statements in the *try* block are ignored. Sometimes, it is necessary to process certain statements, no matter whether an exception is raised or not. The *finally* block is used for this purpose.

Example

```
    try
    {
            openFile( );
            writeFile( );   //may cause an exception
    }
    catch (…)
    {
            //process the exception
    }
```

The file has to be closed irrespective of whether an exception is raised or not. You can place the code to close the file in both the *try* and the *catch* blocks. To avoid rewriting the code, you can place the code in the *finally* block. The code in the *finally* block is executed regardless of whether an exception is thrown or not. The *finally* block follows the *catch* blocks. You can have one *finally* block for an exception-handler, but it is not mandatory to have a *finally* block.

```
Finally
{
        CloseFile( );
}
```

COMMON EXCEPTIONS:

Java has several predefined exceptions. The most common exceptions that you may encounter are described below:

The ArithmeticException Exception:

This exception is throws when an exceptional arithmetic condition has covered. For example, a division by zero generates such an exception.

The NUllPointerException Exception:

This exception is thrown when an application attempts to use null where an object is required. An object that has not been allocated memory holds a null value. The situations in which such an exception is thrown include:

- o Using an object without allocating memory for it.
- o Calling the methods of a *null* object.
- o Accessing or modifying the attributes of a *null* object.
- o Using the length of null as if it were an array.

Example:

String s;
s.length( );   generates such an exception.

The ArrayIndexOutOfBoundsException Exception:

This exception is thrown when an attempt is made to access an array element beyond the index of the array. For example, it is thrown when an array has ten elements and you try to access the eleventh element of the array.

Chapter 6: **Applets and Applications**

Objectives:

In this section, you will learn about:
- o The applet class.
- o The life cycle of an applet.
- o The graphics class.
- o The Font class.
- o Passing parameters to applets.
- o Creating an application
- o Converting applets to applications.

THE APPLET CLASS:

The *java.applet* package is the smallest package in the Java API. The *Applet* class is the only class in the package. An applet is automatically loaded and executed when you open a Web Page that contains it. The *Applet* class has over 20 methods that are used to display images, play audio files, and respond when you interact with it.

The applet runs in a Web page that is loaded in a Web browser. The environment of the applet is known as the *context of the applet*. You can retrieve the context using the *getAppletContext( )* method. The life cycle of an applet is implemented using the methods *init( ), stop( ),* and *destroy( ).*

Use *javac* to compile applets and *appletviewer* to execute them. You can view applets in any browser that is Java-enabled.

APPLETS AND HTML

The *APPLET* tag is used to embed an applet in an HTML document. The *APPLET* tag takes zero or more parameters.

THE APPLET Tag

The APPLET tag is written within the BODY tag of an HTML document.
Syntax:
<APPLET
CODE = "name of the class file that extends java.applet.Applet"
CODEBASE ="path of the class file"
HEIGHT = maximum height of the applet, in pixels
WIDTH = maximum width of the applet, in pixels
VSPACE = vertical space between the applet and the rest of the HTML, in pixels
HSPACE = horizontal space between the applet and the rest of the HTML, in pixels
ALIGN = alignment of the applet with respect to the rest of the Web page.
ALT = "alternate text to be displayed if the browser does not support applets"
>
<PARAM NAME="parameter_name" VALUE="value_of_parameter">
<PARAM NAME="parameter_name" VALUE="value_of_parameter">
………
</APPLET>

The most commonly used attributes of the *APPLET* tag are *CODE, HEIGHT, WIDTH, CODEBASE* and *ALT*.

Example:

<APPLET

CODE = "Clock.class"
HEIGHT = 200
WIDTH = 200>

</APPLET>

LIFE CYCLE OF AN APPLET:

You can describe the life cycle of an applet through four methods. These methods are:

o The *init( )* method.
o The *start( )* method.
o The *stop( )* method.
o The *destroy( )* method.

The *init( )* Method: The *init( )* method is called the first time an applet is loaded into the memory of a computer. You can initialize variables, and add components like buttons and check boxes to the applet in the *init( )* method.

The *start( )* Method: The *start( )* method is called immediately after the init( ) method and every time the applet receives focus as aresult of scrolling in the active window. You can use this method when you want to restart a process, such as thread animation, every time the applet receives the focus.

The stop( ) Method: The *stop( )* method is called every time the applet loses the focus. You can use this method to reset variables and stop the threads that are running.

The destroy Method: The *destroy( )* method is called by the browser when the user moves to another page. You can use this method to perform clean-up operations like closing a file.

The Graphics CLASS:

The *Graphics* class is an abstract class that represents the display area of the applet. It is a part of the *java.awt* package. It is used for drawing on the display area of the applet.
The *Graphics* class provides methods to draw a number of graphical figures including,

➢ Text.
➢ Lines.
➢ Circles and ellipses.
➢ Rectangles and polygons.
➢ Images.

A few of the methods are given below:

public abstract void drawString (String test, int x, int y)
public abstract void drawLine (int x1, int y1, int x2, int y2)
public abstract void drawRect (int x1, int y1, int width, int height)

public abstract void fillRect (int x1, int y1, int width, int height)
public abstract void drawOval (int x1, int y1, int width, int height)

You cannot create an object of the *Graphics* class since it is abstract. You can use the method *getGraphics( )* to obtain an object of the class.

PAINTING THE APPLET:

When you scroll to an applet, the screen has to be refreshed to show the new content. Windows handles this by marking the area (rectangle) that has to be refreshed. The area is then *painted* to display the result of scrolling. This is handled by the *update( )* and *paint( )* methods.

The update( ) Method:

The *update( )* method takes a *Graphics* class object as a parameter. When the applet area needs to be redrawn, the Windows System starts the painting process. The *update( )* method is called to clear the screen and calls the *paint( )* method. The screen is then refreshed by the system.

The *paint( )* Method:

The *paint( )* method draws the graphics of the applet in the drawing area. The method is automatically called the first time the applet is displayed on the screen and every time the applet receives the focus. The *paint( )* method can be triggered by invoking the *repaint( )* method.
The *paint( )* method of the applet takes an object of the *Graphics* class as a parameter.

Example-

```
// DisplayApplet.java
// Code to display a string at the coordinate 20, 20 of the applet
import java.applet.*;
import java.awt. *;
public class DisplayApplet extends Applet
{
        public void paint (Graphics g)
        {
                g.drawString("This is displayed by the paint method", 20, 20);
        }
}
```

The *repaint( )* Method:

You can call the *repaint( )* method when you want the applet area to be redrawn. The *repaint()* method calls the *update()* method to signal that the applet has to be updated. The default action of the *update( )* method is to clear the applet area and call the *paint( )* method. You can override the *update( )* method if you do not want the applet area to be cleared.

The following program uses the *paint( )* and *repaint( )* methods to check when the *init( ),start( ),* and *stop( )* methods of an applet are called.

```
import java.applet. *;
import java.awt.*;
public class AppletMethods extends Applet
{
```

```
int initCounter = 0;
int startCounter = 0;
int stopCounter = 0;
int destroyCounter = 0;

public void init( )
{
        initCounter++;
        repaint( );
}
public void start( )
{
        startCounter++;
        repaint( );
}
public void stop( )
{
        stopCounter++;
        repaint( );
}
public void destroy()
{
        destroyCounter++;
        repaint( );

}
public void paint(Graphics g)
{
        g.drawString("init has been invoked " + String.valueOf(initCounter) +
        "times",  20, 20);
        g.drawString("init has been invoked " + String.valueOf(startCounter) +
        "times",  20, 35);
        g.drawString("init has been invoked " + String.valueOf(stopCounter) +
        "times",  20, 50);
        g.drawString("init has been invoked " + String.valueOf(destroyCounter) +
        "times",  20, 65);

}
}
```

CHANGING THE FONT OF AN APPLET

The Font Class: Using the Font class, you can change the font, and its style and point size.

Example:-

The following code snippet displays a string in the Times New Roman font in bold and italic style, and a point size of 14.

```
public void paint(Graphics g)
        {
                Font myFont = new Font("Times New Roman", Font.BOLD + Font.ITALIC, 14);
                g.setFont(myFont);
                g.drawString("This is displayed by the paint method",20, 20);
        }
```

The program creates an object of the *Font* class and passes the name, style, and size of the font as parameters. The font is applied to the applet using the *setFont( )* method of the *Graphics* class. The *drawString( )* method displays the string in the font applied.

THE AppletContext INTERFACE:

The *Applet* class does not have the capability to change the Web page being display by the browser. *AppletContext* is a link to the browser, and controls the browser environment in which the applet is displayed. Use the *getAppletContext( )* method to retrieve the context of the applet.

        public AppletContextgetAppletContext( );

Use the showStatus( ) method to change the message that is displayed on the status bar of the browser.

        public void showStatus( );

Use the showDocument( ) method to change to another Web page.

        public void showDocument(URL);

The following program illustrates the use of these methods.

```
import java.applet.*;
import java.awt.*;
import java.net. *;
public class ShowDocument extends Applet
{
        public void init( )
        {
                getAppletContext( ).showStatus("Connecting to myWebsite.com...");
                try
                {
                getAppletContext ().showDocument(new URL(http://www.myWebsite.com));
                }
                catch(MalformedURLExcceptionurlException)
                {
                        getAppletContext( ).showStatus("Error connecting to URL");
                }
        }

}
```

The above program displays the *www.myWebsite.com* Web page when the applet is loaded. If the URL is not locatable, an error message is displayed on the status bar of the browser.

URL stands for Uniform Resource Locator. A URL specifies the location of a Web page.

CREATING AN APPLICATION:

All applets must extend from the Applet class. Unlike applets, applications need not be extended from any class. An application does not require a browser for execution.

An application starts with the *main ( )* method. The prototype of the method is as follows:

```
public static void main (String args[ ])
{

}
```

The keywords *public* and *static* can be interchanged in the declaration of the method. Use *javac* to compile a Java application and *java* to execute it.

Passing Parameters to an Application:

You can pass parameters to an application when you execute it. The parameters you send are received as a *String* array. The following code displays the parameters received by the application.

```
public class ParameterApplication
{
        public static void main(string args[] )
        {
                for(int x = 0; x <args.length; x++)
                        System.out.println("Parameter number " + x +" is "+ args[x]);

        }

}
```

Output:

Execute the application with the following statement:

> *java ParameterApplication* Sending five words as parameters

The output is:

    Parameter number 0 is Sending
    Parameter number 1 is five
    Parameter number 2 is words
    Parameter number 3 is as
    Parameter number 4 is parameters

USER-DEFINED EXCEPTIONS:

You can create exception classes by extending the Exception class. The extended class contains constructors, data members, and methods like any other class. The throw and throws keywords are used while implementing user-defined exceptions.

Example

```
//ThrowExample.java
class IllegalValueException extends Exception
{
```

```
}
class UserTrial
{
        int val1, val2;
        public UserTrial(int a, int b)
        {
                val1 = a;
                val2 = b;
        }
        void show( ) throws IllegalValueException
        {
                if ( val1 < 0) || ( val2 > 0)
                        throw new IllegalValueException( );
                System.out.println("Value 1 = " + val1);
                System.out.println("Value 2 = " + val2);
        }
}
class ThrowExample
{
        public static void main (String args[ ] )
        {
                UserTrial  values =  new UserTrial(-1, 1);
                try
                {
                        values.show( );
                }
                catch (IllegalValueException e)
                {
                    System.out.println("Illegal  Values: caught in main");
                }
        }
}
```

An explanation for the above code is given below:

- ➤ In the code given above, a class called *IllegalValueException* is extended from the *Exception* class.
- ➤ The *UserTrial* class has a method that throws a user-defined exception called *IllegalValueException*.
- ➤ The *main()* method in the *ThrowExample* class creates an object of the class *UserTrial* and passes erroneous values to the constructor.
- ➤ The *try( )* block of the *main( )* method invokes the *show( )* method.
- ➤ The *show( )* method throws an *exception*, which is caught by the exception-handles in the *main( )* method.
- ➤ The message present in the *catch* block, "*Illegal values: Caught in main*", is displayed on the screen.

Chapter 7: Using AWT in Applications

In this section you will learn about:
- ➢ The Abstract Window Toolkit
- ➢ The *Component* class.
- ➢ The *Container* class.
- ➢ The *Frame* class.
- ➢ The *Dialog* class.
- ➢ The *Panel* class.
- ➢ Controls.
- ➢ Classes used for controls.
- ➢ Menus.
- ➢ The URL class.
- ➢ The Image classes.
- ➢ The MediaTracker class.

USER INTERFACE:

A user interface is an effective means of making applications user-friendly. It is typically used by organizations for accepting orders from customers or obtaining feedback on their products. You can also conduct tests over the Internet using forms. There are two types of interfaces- Character User Interface (CUI) and Graphical User Interface (GUI).

Using CUI, you interact with the system by keying in commands. You need to remember all the commands and their complete syntax. An example of a CUI operating system is MS-DOS. Today, GUI have been accepted as a worldwide standard for software applications. They provide a 'picture-oriented" or "graphical" way of interacting with the system. The windows family of products is an example of operating systems that support GUI.

The Abstract Window Toolkit:

The abstract Window Toolkit (AWT) is a package that provides an integrated set of classes to manage user interface components like windows, dialog boxes, buttons, check boxes, lists, menus, scrollbars, and text fields. Top-level windows, visual controls such as text boxes and push buttons, as well as simple elements for drawing images on the screen have similar functionality. The component class, which implements the common functionality, is the super class for all graphical interface elements.

COMPONENTS:

The methods of the *component* class allow you to control the internal state and on-screen appearance of all the components.

Features of Component class:

All components are implemented as subclass of the *component* class. The subclasses inherit a large amount of functionality from the *Component* class. The feature of the *Component* class are:

1. Basic Drawing Support

The *Component* class provides the *paint(), update()*, and *repaint()* methods which enable components to be drawn on the screen.

2. Event-Handling

A component is capable of delegating its events (like a mouse click) to other classes for processing.

3. Appearance Control

The Component class provides methods for getting information about the current font and changing the font. It also provides methods to get and set the foreground and background color. The foreground color is the color used for the text displayed in the component as well as for any custom drawing that the component executes. The background color is the color behind the text.

4. Image-Handling

The Component class provides an implementation of the *ImageObserver* interface and defines methods to help components display images.

5. CONTAINERS

Some components can also act as *containers*. A window, for example, can be a part of another container. At the same time, since it can be a parent to other components, such as a text box and a check box, it is a container as well. The *container* class is a special subclass of the *Component* class.

A container contains zero or more components. These components are called *siblings*, since they have the same parent window. There are three main types of containers – *Window, Applet*, and *Panel*. There are two types of windows- *Frame and Dialog*. A frame is a rectangular box with a title and resize buttons. A dialog box is similar to a frame but does not have a menu bar and cannot be resized.

The Frame Class

A frame is a powerful feature of AWT. You can create a window for your application using the *frame* class. A frame has a title bar, an optional menu bar, and a resizable borer. As it is derived from *java.awt.Container*, you can add components to a *frame* using *add( )* method. The *Border layout* is the default layout of the frame. A frame receives mouse events, keyboard events, and focus events.

The constructor of the Frame class receives the title of the frame as a parameter. The string is displayed on the title of the frame.

Frame frame = new Frame("Frame Window");

After the window is created, it can be displayed by calling the *setVisible( )* method. The window can be sized by calling the *setSize( )* method. The following program display a frame.

```
import java.awt. *;

public class frame extends Frame
{
        public static void main(String args[]
        {
                Frame frame;
                frame = new Frame("My Frame");
                frame.setSize(300,400);
                frame.setBackground(Color.red);
                frame.setVisible(true);
        }
}
```

6. The Dialog Class

Dialog are pop-up windows that are used to accept input from user. There are two kinds of dialog boxes- *modal* and *modeless*. Unlike a modeless dialog box, a modal dialog box does not allow a user to interact with other Windows while it is displayed. A dialog must be owned by a frame or another dialog. You cannot directly attach a dialog to an applet. You can attach a dialog to a frame.

When you create a dialog box, you can specify whether you want a modal or a modeless dialog box. You cannot change the "modality" of the dialog box after creating it. Use the *Dialog* class for creating *dialog* boxes. The *Dialog* class offers overloaded constructors.

The following constructors create a dialog box that has another dialog box as its owner.

- o Dialog(Dialog owner_dialog)
- o Dialog(Dialog owner_dialog, String title)
- o Dialog(Dialog owner_dialog, String title, boolean modal)

The following constructors create a dialog box that has another dialog box as its owner.

- o Dialog(Frameowner_frame)
- o Dialog(Frameowner_frame, String title)
- o Dialog(Frameowner_frame, String title, Boolean modal)

The single argument constructor creates a modeless dialog box without a title. The second argument that may be passed to the dialog box constructor is the title of the dialog box. To create a modal dialog, use the three-argument constructor as shown below:
Dialog dialog = new Dialog(frame, "Title of Dialog", true);

The Panel Class:

Panel are used for organizing components. Each panel can have a different layout. To create a panel, give the following command:
Panel panel = new Panel();
Once you have created the panel, add it to a window, a frame, or an applet. This can be done using the *add( )* method of the *Container* class.

Sub-Panels:

You can also create nested panels, with one panel containing one or more panels. You can nest panels as many levels deep as you like. For instance:

Panel mainpanel, subpanel1, subpanel2;
mainpanel = new Panel( );
subpanel1 = new Panel( );
subpanel2 = new Panel();

mainpanel.add(subpanel1);
mainpanel.add(subpanel2);

COMPONENTS AND CONTROLS

Controls:

An integral part of any programming language is the ability to accept data from a user. The user has to be prompted for data entry. To simplify user interaction and make data entry easier, you can use controls. Controls are components, like buttons and text boxes that can be added to containers like frames, panels, and applets.

Controls in java

Control	Function
Text box	Accepts single line alphanumeric entry.
Text area	Accepts multiple line alphanumeric entry.
Push button	Triggers a sequence of action.
Label	Display text.
Check box	Accepts data that has a yes/no value. More than one check box can be selected.
Radio button	Similar to a check box except that it allows the user to select a single option from a group.
Combo box	Display a drop-down list for single item selection. It allows a new value to be entered.
List box	Similar to a combo box except that it allows a user to select single or multiple items. New value cannot be entered.

Classes Involved:-

Controls	Class
Text box	TextField
Text area	TextArea
Push button	Button
Label	Label
Check box	CheckBox
Radio button	CheckboxGroup with CheckBox
Combo box	Choice
List box	List

Adding a Control to a Container

In order to add a control to a container, you need to perform the following two steps:

o   Create an object of the control by passing the required arguments to the constructor.
o   Add the component (control) to the container.

The TextField and TextArea Classes

To accept textual data from a user, AWT provide two classes, *TextField* and *TextArea*. The *TextField* class handles a single line of *TextComponent*class.

Setting a Password Character:

The *TextField* class allows you to specify an echo character that helps you accept a password without displaying what the user has keyed in. For example, if you have specified '*' as the echo character, and the user types in six characters, '******' is display in the text field instead of the text the user has keyed in. Use the *setEchoChar( )* method to set the echo character.

Syntax:

>   setEchoChar(chareChar);

Modifying Text: Text areas have certain special methods that allow you to append, modify, and replace text. To add text at the end of a string, use the method:

>   *public void append (String aText)*

To insert text at a particular position, use the method:

>   *public void insert(StringnText, int pos)*

To replace text at a particular position, use the method:

>   *public void replaceRange(String rText, int start, int end)*

Adding Text Fields to Containers: The following code create a TextField object:

>   *TextFieldtextfield; //* declare an object of the TextField type

>   *Textfield = new TextField(); //* allocate memory

The above statement will call the empty constructor. The constructor will create an empty text field with an unspecified number of columns. To create a text field with a specified number of columns, use the single argument constructor that takes the number of columns as the parameter.

Syntax:
>   **<textfield_object> = new TextField(int numColumn)**

Example:
>   Textfield = new TextField(10);

To initialize the text field with text, the syntax is:

>   **Textfield_object = new TextField(String <initial Text>);**

Example: **Textfield = new TextField("Text field text");**
Use the add( ) method to add the text field to the frame.
>   *Add(textfield);*

Method	Description
String getText( )	Extracts text from the text field.
void setText(String str)	Sets the text of the text field to the text specified in *str*.
void setEchoChar(char c)	Sets the echo character for the field. When the user types anything in the text field, the echo character is displayed.
booleanechoCharIsSet()	Returns *true* if the field is set for echo.
char getEchoChar( )	Return the echo character for the field.
int getColumns( )	Returns the number of columns in the field.
void setEditable(boolean editable)	Makes the field editable, if *true* is passed as the argument.

Adding Text Area to Container:

Adding a text area to a container is similar to adding text field.

TextAreatextarea;
textarea = new TextArea( );
add(textarea);

To create a text area with five rows and six columns, the command is:

textarea = new TextArea(5,6);

To create a text area with a initial value, the command is:

textarea = new TextArea("First text area");

The above example will initialize the text area with a string "*First text area*".

The Label class:

Label do not generate an action event.
Syntax:
Label label = new Label(<label name>, alignment)

The text in the label can be aligned to the left, the right or the centre of the label. The values for alignment are *Label.LEFT, Label.RIGHT, or Label.CENTER*.

Example:

Label label = new Label("Name");

To align the text to the center, use:

Label label = new Label("Name", Label.CENTER);

The Button Class:

Buttons are used to trigger events in a GUI environment. They are easy to manage and, most importantly, they are easy to use. The *Button* class is used to create buttons.

Adding a Button to a Container

Button button = new Button("Button 1");
add(button);

The above code adds a button with the caption "*Button 1*" to a container.

You can use the *setLabel( )* method to change the caption of the button, and the *getLabel( )* method to retrieve the caption.

Syntax:

String s = button.getLabel( );

Example:

public static void main(String args[ ])

{

Frame frame;
Panel panel;
Button button1, button2, button3;
frame = new Frame("My Frame");

```
        frame.setSize(300,400);
        frame.setBackground(Color.blue);
        frame.setVisible(true);


        panel = new Panel( );
        button1 = new Button("Button 1");
        button2 = new Button("Button 2");
        button3 = new Button("Button 3");


        frame.add(panel);
        panel.add(button1);
        panel.add(button1);
        panel.add(button1);
}
```

The Choice Class:

A *choice menu* is used to display a list of choices for the user to select from. When the user clicks on the choice control, a list of options drops down. The choice menu allows a user to key in a value that does not exist in the list of options provided.

Adding the Choice Menu to a Container

> *Choice choice = new Choice( );*
> *Add(choice);*

The *Choice( )* class constructor does not take an argument. You can add items to the menu by calling the *addItem( )* method of the class.

> *Choice.addItem("Option 1");*

You can call the *addItem( )* method as often as needed to build a complete menu. You can use an array of strings and a *for* loop to accomplish this.

```
import java.awt.*;
public class choice
{
        public static void main(String args[ ])
        {
                Frame frame;
                Panel panel;
                Choice ch;
                frame = new Frame("My Frame");
                frame.setVisible(true);
                frame.setSize(300,300);
                panel = new Panel( );
                frame.add(panel);
                ch = new Choice( );
                ch.addItem("Choice 1");
```

```
                ch.addItem("Choice 2");
                ch.addItem("Choice 3");
                panel.add(ch);
        }
}
```

The List Class:

The *List* class allows you to create a scrolling list of values. You can enable single or multiple selection using a list. The user only needs to double-click on an item to make the selection. The code for creating a list is:

> *List list = new List(num, val);*

The arguments to the constructor are the number of visible lines in the list and a *boolean* value indicating whether the list supports multiple-selection list. The *boolean* value *false* indicates a single-selection list and the *boolean* value *true* indicates a multiple-selection list.

> *List list = new List(10, true);*

The above code creates a list box that allows a maximum of ten options simultaneously and allows multiple selection. You can add items to the list box using add( ) method.

> *list.add("Option 1");*

You can also add items at a specified location in the list. Consider the following:

> list.add(str, 0);

The Checkbox Class:

The *Checkbox* class is used to create a labeled check box. A check box has two parts – a label and a state. The label is the text that represents the caption of the control and the state is the *boolean* value that represents the status of the check box. The check box returns a *boolean*value(true or false). By default, the state is *false* which means that the check box is *unchecked*.

To create a check box, you call the constructor of the Checkbox class.

> *Checkbox cb = new Checkbox(str, group, check);*

in which:

str – is the text string for the label of the check box.

group – is a reference to a *CheckboxGroup* object (used only for exclusive check boxes).

check- is a *boolean* value indicating whether a check box is *checked(true)* or *unchecked (true)* or *unchecked(false)*.

After the check box is created, you add the check box to the container using the add( ) method.

The CheckboxGroup Class:

Check box groups are also called *radio buttons or exclusive check boxes*. In order to create a list of exclusive check boxes, you need to first associate the check boxes in the list with a *CheckboxGroup* object. The first step is to create the *CheckboxGroup* object using the following code:

CheckboxGroupradioGroup = new CheckboxGroup( );

The constructor of the *CheckboxGroup* class takes no arguments. After you create the *CheckboxGroup* object, create the check boxes by giving a reference to the *CheckboxGroup* object as the second argument *Checkbox* constructor.

cb1 = new Checkbox("101 Dalmations", radioGroup, true);
cb2 = new Checkbox("Pochahontas", radioGroup, false);
cb3 = new Checkbox("Pochahontas", radioGroup, false);

In the above code, all the check boxes – *cb1, cb2,* and *cb3* are part of the same group named "*radioGroup*". It will allow the user to select any one option from the group. To add the check boxes to the container, call the *add( )* method.

add(cb1);
add(cb1);
add(cb1);

MENUS:

Most Windows application have menu bars that enable users to easily locate and select various commands and options supported by the program. There are two kinds of menus supported by Java – regular menus and pop-up menus. Java provides the following classes for creating and managing menus.

- o MenuBar
- o Menu
- o MenuItem
- o CheckboxMenuItem

Creating Regular Menus:

Steps for creating regular menus:

1. Create an objective of the *MenuBar* class.
   You can attach a *MenuBar* class to a frame. The menu bar in a window is the horizontal area below the title bar of the window, and contains the caption of each menu. The *MenuBar*object is created as shown below:
   MenuBar bm = new MenuBar( );

2. Call the *setMenuBar( )* method of the window to attach the menu bar to the frame.
   setMenuBar(mb);

   An empty menu bar is associated with the frame.

3. Create object of the *Menu* class for each menu you want on the menu bar.

   Menu fileMenu = new Menu("File");

Menu editManu = new Menu("Edit");

Menu optionMenu = new Menu ("Options");

The constructor of the *Menu* class takes a single string argument. The string appears as a caption of the menu on the menu bar. The code given above creates the menu for the menu bar.

4. Call the *add( )* method of the MenuBar class to add each menu object to the menu bar.
   ```
   mb.add(fileMenu);
   mb.add(editMenu);
   mb. Add(optionMenu);
   ```

5. Create objects of the *MenuItem* or *CheckboxMenuItem* class for each sub-menu item. The check box menu item functions like a check box button. The following code adds menu items to the *Options* menu create earlier.

   MenuItem opt1 = new MenuItem("Option 1");
   MenuItem opt2 = new MenuItem("Option 2");
   MenuItemsep = new MenuItem("-");   // Separator
   MenuItem opt3 = new MenuItem("Option 3");

   The following code creates a check box menu item:

   CheckboxMenuItem opt4 = new CheckboxMenuItem("option 4");

6. Call the add( ) method of the Menu class to add each menu item to its appropriate menu.

   optionMenu.add(opt1);
   optionMenu.add(opt2);
   optionMenu.add(sep);
   optionMenu.add(opt3);

Example:

```
import java.awt.*;
public class MyMenu
{
        public static void main(String args[ ])
        {
                // Create a frame and a menubar
                Frame frame;
                MenuBar mb;
                frame = new Frame("My frame");
                mb = new MenuBar( );
                //Add the menubar to the frame
                frame.setMenuBar(mb);

                // Create the file & the Edit Menus, attach it to menubar.
```

```java
        Menu mFile,mEdit;
        mFile = new Menu("File");
        mEdit = new Menu("Edit");
        mb.add(mFile);
        mb.add(mEdit);

// Add New and Close options to file menu
// Add Copy and Paste to the Edit menu

        MenuItemmNew, mClose, mCopy, mPaste;
        mNew = new Menu("New");
        mClose = new Menu("Close");
        mCopy = new Menu("Copy");
        mFile.add(mNew);
        mFile.add(mClose);
        mEdit.add(mCopy);
        mEdit.add(mPaste);

        // Make Close disabled
        mClose.setEnabled(false);

        // Resize the frame
        frame.setSize(400, 400);

        // Display the frame on the screen
        frame.setVisible(true);


    }
}
```

Chapter 8: Event-Handling

Objectives:

In this section, you will learn about:

- Events.
- Event-driven Programming.
- Event Listeners.
- Handling an Event.
- Handling Window Events,
- Adapter Classes,
- Inner Classes,
- Anonymous classes.

You are leaving for class in the morning, and the mobile rings ……

That's an *event!*

In life, you encounter events that force you to suspended other activities and respond to them immediately. In Java, events represent all the activities that goes on between the application and its user. When the user interacts with a program (say, by clicking on a command button), the system creates an event representing the action and delegates it to the event-handling code within the program. This code determines how to handle the event so that the user gets the appropriate response.

This chapter explains event-driven programming, the event model of Java, and the different ways in which you can handle events.

EVENT-DRIVEN PROGRMMING:

Event-handling is essential to GUI programming. The program waits for a user to perform some action. The user controls the sequence of operations that the application executes through a GUI. This approach is called event-driven programming.

Components of an Event:

An event comprises of three components:

- o Event object – When the user interacts with the application by pressing a key or clicking a mouse button, an event is generated. The operating system traps this event and the data associated with it, for example, the time at which the event occurred, the event type (like, keypress, or a mouse click). This data is then passed on to the application to which the event belongs.
  In java, events are represented by objects that describe the events themselves. Java has a number of classes that describe and handle different categories of events.
- o Event source – An event source is an object that generates an event. For example, if you click on a button, an *ActionEvent* object is generated. The object of the *ActionEvent* class contains information about the event.
- o Event-handler – An *event-handler* is a method that understands the event and processes it. The event-handler method takes an *Event* object as a parameter.

ActionEvent is a class that contains the *getSource( )* method, which returns the reference to the component that generated the event.

The *getSource( )* method of the *EventObject* class returns the object that initiated the event. The *getID( )* method returns the event ID that represents the nature of the event. For example, if a mouse event occurs, you can find out whether the event was a click, a drag, a move, a press, or a release from the event object.

Event Listeners:

An object delegates the task of handling an event to an *event listener*. When an event occurs, an event object of the appropriate type is created. This object is passed to the listener. A listener must implement the interface that has the method for event-handling. A component can have multiple listeners. A listener can be removed using the *removeActionListener( )* method.

```java
class MyListener implements ActionListener
{
        public void actionPerformed(ActionEvent action)
        {
                //handle the event
        }
}


public class UserListener extends Applet
{
        public void init( )
        {
                Button OK = new Button("OK");
                // Create listener object
                MyListener listen = new MyListener( );
                // delegate events of the button to the listener
                OK.addActionListener(listen);
                // add the button to the applet
                Add(OK);
        }
}
```

Explicit Event-Handling:

An alternate way to handle events is to subclass the component and override the method that receives and dispatches events. For example, you can derive a class from the *Button* class and override the *processActionEvent( )* method. The default action of *the processActionEvent( )* method is to dispatch the event to event listeners.

Example:

```
class OKButton extends Button
{
        public OKButton(String caption)
        {
                Super(caption);
                    // enable processing of action events
                enableEvents(AWTEvent.ACTION_EVENT_MASK);

        }
        public void processActionEvent(ActionEvent action)
        {
                // process event
                // call superclass method as it calls actionPerformed( ) method
                Super.processActionEvent(action);
        }
}
```

A superclass can act as an event listener for itself. When you use interfaces for creating listeners, the listener class has to override all the methods that are declared in the interface. Some of the interfaces have only one method, whereas others have many. Even if you want to handle only one event, you have to override all the methods. To overcome this, the event package provides seven adapter classes.

HANDLING AN EVENT:

When an event occurs, it is sent to the component from where the event originated. The component registers a listener, which contains event-handlers. Event-handlers receive and process events.

Every event has a corresponding listener interface that specifies the methods that are required to handle the event. Event objects are reported to registered listeners. To enable a component to handle events, you must register an appropriate listener for that component.

Example:

```
        // MyFrame.java file

import java.awt.*;
import java.awt.event.*;
class MyFrame extends Frame
{
        Button b1;
// The main method
public static void main(String args[ ])
```

```
{
        MyFrame f =new MyFrame( );
}
// Constructor
        public MyFrame()
        {
                super("Windo Title");
                b1 = new Button("Click Here");
        // Place the button object on the window
                add("Center", b1);

                //Register the listener for the button
                        ButtonListenerblisten = new ButtonListener( );
                        b1.addActionListener(blisten);

        // Display the window in a specific size
                setVisible(true);
                setSize(200,200);
        }
} //end of the Frame class
//The listener class
class ButtonListener implements ActionListener
{
        // Definition of the actionPerformed( ) method
        public void actionPerformed(ActionEventevt)
        {
                Button source = (Button) evt.getSource( );
                source.setLabel(" Button Clicked");
        }
}
```

How does the above application work?

- o The execution begins with the main() method.
- o An object of the MyFrame class is created in the main( ) method.
- o The constructor of the MyFrame class is called.
- o The *super( )* method calls the constructor of the base class9Frame) and sets the title of the window.
- o A button object is created and placed at the center of the window.
- o A listener object is created.
- o The addActionListener( ) method registers the listener object for the button.
- o The setVisible( ) method displays the window.
- o The application waits for the user to interact with it.
- o When the user clicks on the button –
    - The *ActionEvent*event is generated.
    - An *ActionEvent* object is created and is delegated to the registered listener object for processing.

- The listener object contains the actionPerformed( ) method, which processes the ActionEvent.
- In the actioinPerformed( ) method, the reference to the event source is retrived using the getSource( ) method.
- Finally, the label of the button is changed using the setLabel( ) method.

The component that does not have a registered listener cannot handle events.

Handling Window Events:

In order to handle window-related events, you need to register the listener object that implements the *WindowListener* interface. The *WindowListener* interface contains a set of methods that are used to handle window events.

Category	Event	Method
Window events	The user click on the cross button.	void windowclosing(windowEvente)
	The window is opened for the first time.	void windowOpened(windowEvent e)
	The window is activated.	void windowActivated(windowEvent e)
	The window is deactivated.	void windowDeactivated(windowEvent e)
	The window is closed.	void windowClosed(windowEvent e)
	The window is minimized.	void windowIconified(windowEvent e)
	The window is maximized.	void windowDeiconified(windowEvent e)

ADAPTER CLASSES:

The Java programming language provides adapter classes that implement the corresponding listener interface containing more than one method. The methods in these classes are empty. The listener class that you define can extend the *Adapter* class and override the methods that you need. The Adapter class used for the *WindowListener* interface is the *WindowAdapter* class.

You can write the code in the following manner:

```
import java.awt.*;
import java.awt.event.*;
class MyFrame extends Frame
{
        public static void main(String args[ ] )
        {
                MyFrame f = new MyFrame( );
        }
        // Constructor of the Frame derived class
        public MyFrame( )
        {
                // Register the listener for the window
```

```
                super("The window Adapter");
                MyWindowListener  listen = new MyWindowListener( );
                addWindowListener(listen);
                setVisible(true);
        }

}

class MyWindowListener   extends WindowAdapter

{

        // Event handler for the window closing event

        public void windowClosing(WindowEvent w)

        {

                MyFrame f;
                f = (MyFrame)w.getSource( );
                f.dispose( );
                System.exit(0);

        }

}
```

INNER CLASSES:

Inner classes are classes that are declared within other classes. They are also known as nested classes and provide additional clarity to programs. The scope of an inner class is limited to the class that encloses it. The objects of the inner class can access the members of the outer class. The outer class can access the members of the inner class through an object of the inner class.

Syntax:

```
<modifiers> class <classname>

{

        `<modifiers> class <innerclassname>

        {

        }

        // Other attributes and methods

}
```

Example:

```
MyFrame frame = new MyFrame("Title");
frame.MyWindowListener listen= new MyFrame( ).MyWindowListener( );
```

You can also create a class inside a method. The inner class methods can then access the variables defined in the method containing them. The inner class must be declared after the declaration of the variables of the method so that the variables are accessible to the inner class.

ANONYMOUS CLASSES:

Sometimes, the classes that you declare in a method do not need a name since you do not need them anywhere else in the program. You can create nameless classes for this purpose. Classes that are not named are called *anonymous classes*.

Example:

```
public void methodOne( )
{
        OKButton.addActionListener(new ActionListener( )
        {
                public void actionPerformed(ActionEvent action)
                {
                        // process event
                }
        }
        );
}
```

In the above code, the class declaration is the argument of the addActionListener( ) method. You cannot instantiate an object of the anonymous class elsewhere in the code.

An anonymous class cannot have a constructor as the class does not have a name. An anonymous class be a subclass of another class. It can implement an interface.

Chapter 9: **Networking**

Objectives:

In this Section, you will learn about:

- o The client/server model.
- o Protocols.
- o IP addresses.
- o Sockets.
- o The *Socket* class.

THE CLIENT/SERVER MODEL:

In a restaurant, you are greeted by a variety of exotic food on the menu, and you order for a pizza. A few minutes later, you are munching a hot pizza topped with melted cheese and everything else you wanted on it. You do not know, nor do you want to know, where the waiter got the pizza from, what went into its making or how the ingredients were obtained.

What you are looking at is a client/server model. The client places a request or order to the server. The server processes the request of the client. The communication between the client and the server is an important constituent in Client/Server models, and is usually through a *network*.

The Client/server model is an application development architecture designed to separate the presentation of data from its internal processing and storage. The client requests for services and the server services these requests. The requests are transferred from the client to the server over the network. The processing that is done by the server is hidden from the client. One server can service multiple clients.

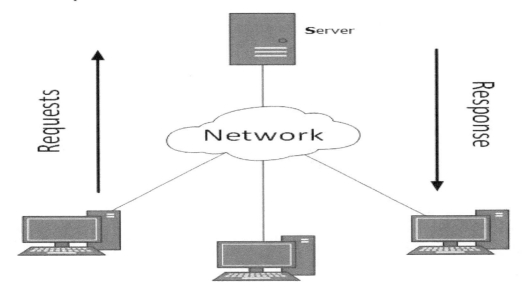

Multiple Clients Accessing a Server

The server and the client are not necessarily hardware components. They can be programs working on the same machine or on different machines.

The server portion of the client/server application manages the resources shared among multiple users who access the server through multiple clients. The best example to highlight the server part of a client/server program would be a Web server that delivers an HTML page across the Internet to different Web uses.

PROTOCOLS:

When you talk to your friend, you follow some implicit rules (or protocol). For example, both of you do not start talking at the same time or talk continuously without a pause. Neither of you would understand what the other person is saying if you were to do so. When you talk, your friend listens and vice-versa. You talk in a language and at a pace that both of you understand.

When computers communicate, they need to follow certain rules too. Data is sent from one machine to another in the form of packets. Rules govern packaging of the data into packets, speed of transmission and recreation of data to its original form. These rules are called *Network protocols*. *Network protocols* are a set of rules and conventions followed by systems that communicate over a network. Networking software usually implements multiple levels of protocols layered one on top of another. Some examples of network protocols are TCP/IP, UDP, Applet talk, and NetBEUI.

Java provides a rich library of network-enabled classes that allow applications to readily access network resources. There are two tools available in Java for communication. These include *datagrams* that are use *User Datagram Protocol* (UDP) and *sockets* that use *Transmission Control Protocol/Internet Protocol* (TCP/IP).

A *datagram packet* is an array of bytes sent from one program (sending program) to another (receiving program). As datagrams follow UDP, there is no guarantee that the data packet sent will reach its destination. Datagrams are not reliable and are, therefore, used only when there is little data to be transmitted, and there is not much distance between the sender and the receiver. If the network traffic is high, or the receiving program is handling multiple requests from other programs, there is a chance of the datagram packet being lost.

Sockets, on the other hand, use TCP for communication. The advantage of the socket model over other communication models is that the server is not affected by the source of client requests. It services all requests, as long as the clients follow the TCP/IP protocols. This means that the client can be any kind of computer. No longer is the client restricted to UNIX, Windows, DOS, or Macintosh platform. Therefore, all the computers in a network implementing TCP/IP can communicate with each other through sockets.

SOCKETS: Overview of Sockets

In client/server applications, the server provides services like processing database queries or modifying data in the database. The communication that occurs between the client and the server must be reliable. The data must not be lost and must be available to the client in the same sequence in which the server sent it.

Transmission control protocol (TCP) provides a reliable, point-to-point communication channel that client/server applications can use to communicate with each other. To communicate over TCP, client and server programs establish a connection and bind a *socket*. Sockets are used to handle communication links between applications over the network. Further communication between the client and the server is through the socket.

Java was designed as a networking language. It makes network programming easier by encapsulating connection functionality in the *Socket* classes. That is, the *Socket* class to create a *client socket*, and the *ServerSocket* class to create a *server socket*. The different socket classes are outlined below:

- *Socket* is the basic class, which supports the TCP protocol. TCP is a reliable stream network connection protocol. The *Socket* class provides methods for stream I/O, which makes reading from and writing to a socket easy. This class is indispensable to the programs written to communicate on the Internet.
- *ServerSocket* is a class used by Internet server programs for listening to client requests.
- *ServerSocket* does not actually perform the service; instead, it creates a *Socket* object on behalf of the client. The communication is performed through the object created.

IP Addresses and Port:

An Internet server can be thought of as a set of socket classes that provide additional capabilities – generally called *services*. Some examples of services are electronic mail, Telnet for remote login, and *File Transfer Protocol* (FTP) for transferring files across the network. Each service is associated with a *port*. A port is a numeric address through which service requests, such as a request for a Web page, are processed.

The TCP protocol requires two data items: the IP address and the port number. So how is it possible that when you type *https://www.oracle.com* you get to Oracle home page?

The *Internet Protocol* (IP) provides every network device with a logical address called an *IP address*. The IP address provided by the Internet protocol take a specific form. Each is a 32-bit number, represented as a series of four 8-bit numbers, which range in value from 0 to 255. Oracle has registered its name, allowing *www.oracle.com to be assigned an IP address.*

If the port number is not specified, the server's port in the services file is used. Every protocol has a default port number, which is used if the port number is not specified.

Port Number	Application
21	FTP, which transfers files
23	Telnet, which provides a remote login.
25	SMTP, which delivers mail messages.
67	BOOTP, which provides configuration at boot time.
80	HTTP, which transfer Web pages.
109	POP, which enables users to access mail boxes on remote systems.

First part of the URL (http) means that you are using *HyperText Transmission Protocol(HTTP)*, the protocol for handling Web documents. If a file is not specified, most Web servers are configured to fetch the file called index.html. Therefore, the IP address and the port are determined either by explicit specification of all the parts of the URL or by using the default.

Creating a Socket:

Creating a TCP connection to a server involves the following code segment:

```
Socket socketConnection;
try
{
        socketConnection = new Socket("www.oracle.com",1001);
}
catch(IOException e)
```

```
{

}
```

The constructor for the *socket* class requires a host to connect to, in this case www.oracle.com, and a port number 1001, which is the port of a server. If the server is up and running, the code creates a new *Socket* instance and continues running. If the code encounters a problem while connecting, it throws an exception. The disconnect from the server, use the *close ()* method.

socketConnection.close();

Importing Packages:

Import the necessary packages for networking in Java using the import stamen.

import java.net. *;
import java.io. *;

CREATING A SOCKET CLIENT:

Creating a Socket Class Object-

The first step to create a socket client is to create a *Socket* object. The constructor of the Socket class takes two parameters- the IP address and the port number at which the server listens.

Socket clientSocket = new Socket("www.oracle.com",1001);

Here, in the above code snippet, the host name is www.oracle.com and the port number 1001 is the port at which the server listens.

Reading from and writing to the Socket

Reading from and writing to a socket is similar to reading from and writing to files. Declare two objects, one each of the *PrintStream* and *BufferedReader* classes. The objects will be used for reading and writing to the socket.

CREATING A SOCKET CLIENT:

Creating a Socket Class Object-

The first step to create a socket client is to create a *Socket* object. The constructor of the *Socket* class takes two parameters – the IP address and the port number at which the server listens.

Socket clientSocket = new Socket("www.oracle.com",1001);

Here, in the above code snippet, the host name is *www.oracle.com* and the port number 1001 is the port at which the server listens.

Reading from and Writing to the Socket:

Reading from and writing to a socket is similar to reading from and writing to files. Declare two objects, one each of the *PrintStream* and *BufferedReader* classes. These objects will be used for reading and writing to the socket.

PrintStream out = null;   // To write to the socket

BufferedReader in = null;   //To read from the socket

Associate the PrintStream and BufferedReader objects to the socket.

out = new PrintStream(clientSocket.getOutputStream());

in = new BufferedReader(new InputStreamReader(clientSocket.getInputStream( ));

The *getInputStream*( ) and the *getOutputStream*( ) methods of the Socket class enable a client to communicate with the server. The *getInputStream*( ) method is used for reading from the socket and the *getOutputStream*( ) method is used for writing to a socket.

Declare another object of the *BufferedReader* class to associate with the standard input, so that the data entered at the client can be sent to the server.

BufferedReader stdin = new BufferedReader(new InputStreamReader(System.in));

String str;

```
while (str = stdin.readLine( ) ).length( ) ! = 0 )
{
        System.out.println(str);
}
```

The above code allows a user to accept data from the keyboard. The while loop continues until the user types an end-of-input character.

Closing the Connection:

The statements given below close the streams and the connection to the server.

```
out.close( );
in.close( );
stdin.close( );
```

The following program code terminate the connection when the client has entered 'Bye'.

```
System.out.println(str);
while (str = stdin.readLine( ) ).length( ) ! = 0 )
{
        out.println(str);
        if(str.equals("Bye"))
                Break;
}
out.close( );
in.close( );
stdin.close( );
```

CREATE A SERVER SOCKET:

Classes Used by the Server:

To create a server, you need to create a *ServerSocket* object that listens at a particular port for client requests. When it recognizes a valid request, the server socket obtains the Socket object created by the client. The communication between the server and the client occurs using this socket.

Use the ServerSocket class of the *java.net* package to create a socket where the server listens for remote login requests. Use the *IOException* class to handle errors from the *java.io* package. The *BuffedReader* class handles data transfer from the client to the server. The *PrintStream* class handles the transfer of data from the server to the client.

A server socket waits for requests to come in over the network. It performs operations based on a request, and returns the result to the client. The *ServerSocket* class represents the server ina client/server application. The *ServerSocket* class provides constructors to create a socket on a specified port. A value of zero passed as an argument for a port creates the socket on a free port.

Besides, the class provides methods which:

- o Listen for a connection.
- o Return the address and local port.
- o Return a string representation of the socket.

The two-argument constructor takes the port number, i.e., the port at which all the client requests will be serviced, and the second argument specifies the maximum number of connections available. The *toString( )* method returns information on the socket created. The information contains the IP address, the port and the local port on which the socket is created. The *close( )* method closes the socket. Both the constructor and the *close( )* method throw an *IOException* that has to be caught and handled.

Note:

To get the IP address of the network that you are working on, call the *getLocalHost( )* and *getAddress( )* methods of the class *java.net.InetAddress( )* method. First, the method *getLocalHost( )* returns an *InetAddress*object. Then, use the getAddress( ) method, which returns a byte array consisting of the four bytes of the IP address, as in the following example:

InetAddresslocal_address = InetAddress.getLocalHost( ) ;

byte[] ipaddress = local_address.getAddress( ) ;

If the IP address of the network is 43.111.112.23, then

ipaddress[0] = 43

ipaddress[1] = 111

ipaddress[2] = 112

ipaddress[3] = 23

The *accept( )* method waits for a client connection by listening to the port to which it is bound. When a client attempts to the server socket, the method accepts the connection and returns a client socket. The socket is later used for communication between the server and its client. The output stream of this socket is the input stream for the connection client and vice versa. An *IOException* is shown if any error occurs while establishing the connection. Java forces you to handle the exceptions raised.

Creating the Server:

The *Server* class is a subclass of the *Thread* class. A *ServerSocket* object listens for client requests. The constructor of the *Server* class creates and starts a *ServerSocket* thread. An error message is displayed if an exception is thrown when starting the server.

The code for the constructor is given below:

```
public Server ( )
{
        try
        {
                serverSocket = new ServerSocket(1001);
        }
        catch(IOException e)
        {
                fail(e, "Could not start server");
        }
        System.out.println("Server started ....");
        this.strat();              // starts the thread
}
```

In this program, a common error-handling routine called *fail( )* is defined to take care of all exception-handling. It takes two arguments (an Exception object and a *Strating* object), prints an error message and exits. The code for the routine is as follows:

Listening for a Client's Request:

The *run( )* method of the server, as with all threads that implement the *Runnable* interface, has the instructions for the thread. In this case, the server goes into an infinite loop and listens for client requests. When the server secures a connection from the client, the *accept( )* method of the *ServerSocket* class accepts the connection. The server creates an object of the user-defined class *Connection* for the client, passing a *Socket* object to the constructor. Communication between the client and the server occurs through this socket. The code for the *run( )* method is given below:

```
public void run( )
{
        try
        {
                while(true)
                {
                        Socket client = ServerSocket.accept();
                        Connection con = new Connection(client);
                }
        }
```

```
catch (IOException e)
{
        Fail ( e, "Not listening");
}
}
```

Starting the Server:

The code for the *main( )* method is given below. It creates an object of the Server class that starts the thread.

```
public static void main(String args[])

{

        new Server( );

}
```

Connection Thread:

The *Connection* class creates a *BufferedReader* object (*fromClient*), which retrieves input from the client using the *getInputStream( )* method, and a *PrintStream* object (*toClient*) which enables the server to write to the client using the *getOutputStream( )* method. Thus, a two-way communication occurs.

The server is multi-threaded, and each client gets ite own thread in the server.

Chapter 10: Java Database Connectivity:

Establishing a Connection (JDBC, ODBC connectivity), transactions with database.

In this section, you will learn about:
- ➢ Database management.
- ➢ Database connectivity.
  - ODBC API.
  - JDBC API.
  - Installing the ODBC driver.
- ➢ Querying a database.
  - The *Statement*object.
  - The *PreparedStatement* object.
  - Retrieving and processing a *ResultSet* object.
- ➢ Adding, modifying, and deleting records.

Most of the Web-based application programs need to interact with database management systems (DBMS). These DBMSs are repositories of the information used by applications. For example, an online shopping mall needs to keep track of its customers and the items sold. A search site like *www.google.com* needs to keep track of the URLs of the Web pages visited by the user.

This section explains the techniques of database programming using Java. You will also see how databases are accessed using the JDBC-ODBC bridge and ODBC drivers.

DATABASE MANAGEMENT:

A *database* is a collection of related information and a DBMS is a software that provides you with a mechanism to retrieve, modify, and add data to the database. There are many DBMS/RDBMS products available, for example, MS-Access, MS-SQL Server, Oracle, Sybase, Informix, Progress, and Ingres. Each of these *Relational Database Management System* (RDBMS) stores data in its own format. For example, MS-Access stores data in the .MDB file format, whereas MS-SQL Server stores data in the .DAT file format.

DATABASE CONNECTIVITY:

For your application to communicate with the database, it needs to have the following information:

- o The RDBMS/DBMS product using which the database is created.
- o The location of the database.
- o The name of the database.

The application you created would be able to work with only one kind of database and will be very difficult to code and port.

The above problem is solved by Microsoft's standard for communicating with database called *Open Database Connectivity* (ODBC).

ODBC Application Programming Interface (API):

ODBC API is a set of library routines that enable your programs to access a variety of databases. All you need to do is to install a DBMS-specific ODBC driver and write your program to interact with the specified ODBC driver.

Later, if the database is upgraded to a newer version of RDBMS or ported to a different RDBMS product, you will need to change only the ODBC driver and not the program.

INSTALLING THE ODBC DRIVER:

Open Database Connectivity (ODBC) is a standard application programming interface that allows external applications to access data from diverse database management systems. The ODBC interface provides for maximum interoperability – an application that is independent of any DBMS, can access data in various databases through a tool called an ODBC driver, which serves as an interface between an external program and an ODBC data source, i.e. a specific DBMS or cloud service.

The ODBC driver connection string is a parameterized string that consists of one or more name-value pairs separated by semi-colons. Parameters may include information about the data source name, server address and port, username and password, security protocols, SQL dialects, and many more. The required information is different depending on the specific driver and database. Here's an example of ODBC connection string:

DRIVER={Devart ODBC Driver for Oracle};Direct=True;Host=127.0.0.1;SID=ORCL1020;User ID=John;Password=Doe

Installing ODBC Driver for Windows:-

1. Run the downloaded installer file. If you already have another version of the driver installed in the system, you will get a warning — click Yes to overwrite the old files, though it's recommended to first uninstall the old version. If this is the first time you install Devart ODBC driver, just click Next.

2.Read and accept the license agreement, then click Next.

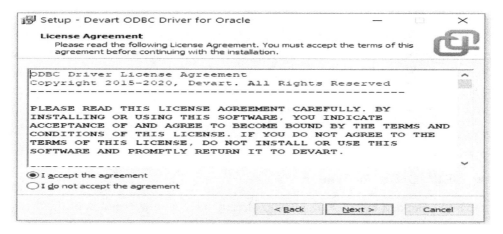

3. Select the installation directory for the ODBC driver and click Next.

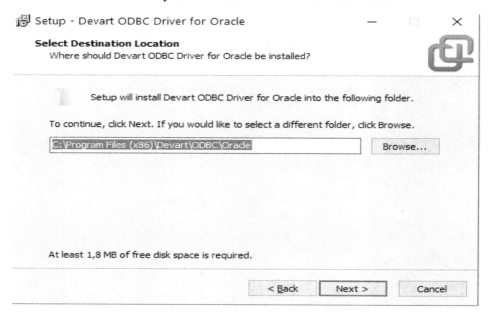

4. In the Select Components tab, select which version of the driver to install (64-bit / 32-bit), and whether to include the help files.

5. Confirm or change the Start Menu Folder and click Next.

6. Input your activation key or choose Trial if you want to evaluate the product before getting a license. You can load the activation key by clicking on the Load Activation Key... button and selecting the license file from your machine. Click Next and then Install.

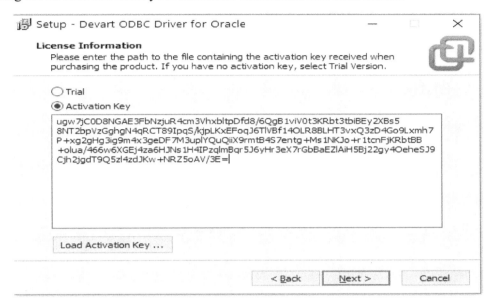

After the installation is completed, click Finish.

How to Configure Data Source Name (DSN) for the ODBC driver on Windows:

Before connecting a third-party application to a database or cloud source through ODBC, you need to set up a data source name (DSN) for the ODBC driver in the Data Source Administrator. A 64-bit version of the Microsoft Windows operating system includes both the 64-bit and 32-bit versions of the Open Database Connectivity (ODBC) Data Source Administrator tool (odbcad32.exe):

1. The 32-bit version of odbcad32.exe is located in the C: \Windows\SysWoW64 folder.
2. The 64-bit version of odbcad32.exe is located in the C: \Windows\System32 folder.

1. In your Windows Search bar, type ODBC Data Sources. The ODBC Data Sources (64 bit) and ODBC Data Sources (32 bit) apps should appear in the search results.

Alternatively, you can open the Run dialog box by pressing Windows+R, type odbcad32 and click OK.

Yet another way to open the ODBC Data Source Administrator is via the command prompt: enter cmd in the search bar and click the resulting Command Prompt button. Enter the command odbcad32 and hit Enter.

2. Since most modern computer architectures are 64-bit, we'll select the 64-bit version of the ODBC Data Source Administrator to create a DSN for our ODBC driver. The odbcad32.exe file displays two types of data source names: System DSNs and User DSNs. A User DSN is only accessible to the user who created it in the system. A System DSN is accessible to any user who is logged in into the system. If you don't want other users on the workstation to access your data source using the DSN, choose a User DSN.

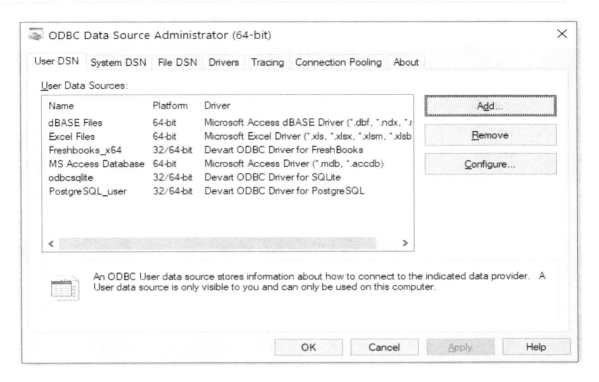

3. In the administrator utility, click the Add button. The Create New Data Source dialog box will display the list of installed ODBC drivers in the system. Choose the needed driver from the list. The choice of the driver is determined by the data source you are trying to connect to — for example, to access a PostgreSQL database, choose Devart OBDC Driver for PostgreSQL. Click Finish.

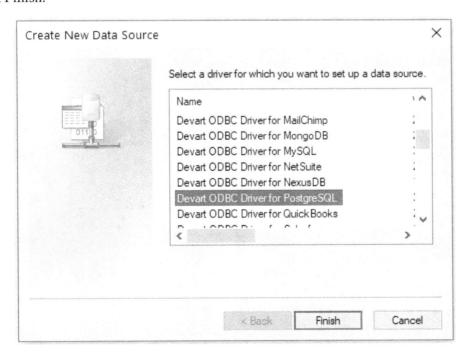

4. Enter a name for your data source in the corresponding field. Fill in the parameters for the ODBC connection string, which is driver-specific. In most of our ODBC drivers for databases, a connection string with basic parameters requires the user to only input their server address, port

number, and login credentials, since Devart ODBC drivers allow direct access to the database without involving additional client libraries.

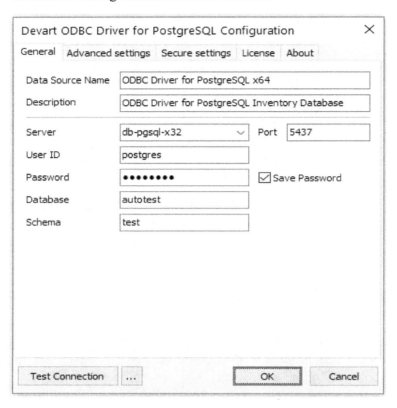

5. Click Test Connection to verify connectivity. If you see the Connection Successful message, click OK to save the DSN. You should now see your new DSN in the User DSN tab of the ODBC Data Source Administrator tool.

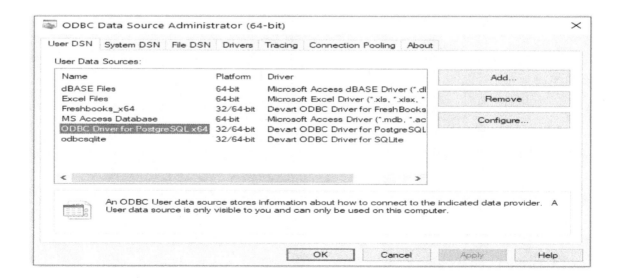

How to Test ODBC Connection:

Ensure your ODBC driver is functioning correctly by performing the following steps:

1. Open the "ODBC Data Source Administrator."
2. Switch to the "User DSN" or "System DSN" tab, depending on where your data source is configured.
3. Select the configured data source and click the "Configure" or "Test Connection" button.
4. Follow the on-screen instructions to test the ODBC connection.
5. Once the test is complete, a success message will indicate that the ODBC connection is working.

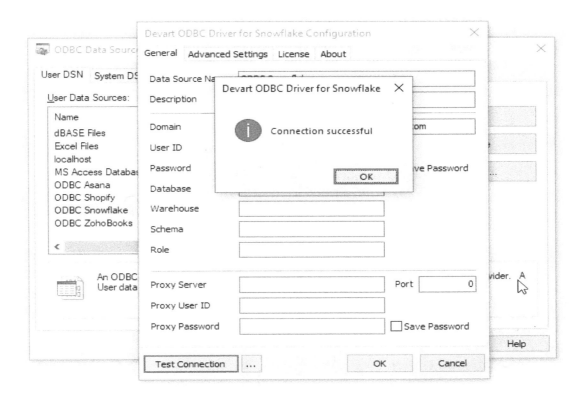

QUERYING A DATABASE:

Now that you have understood the JDBC architecture, you can write a Java Application that is capable of working with a database. In this section you will learn about packages and classes available in Java that allow you to send queries to a database and process query results.

Connecting to a Database

The *java.sql* package contains classes that help in connecting to a database, sending embedded SQL statements to the database, and processing query results.

The Connection Objects

The *Connection* object represents a connection with a database. You may have several *Connection* objects in an application that connects to one or more database.

Loading the JDBC-ODBC Bridge and Establishing the Connection

To establish a connection with a database, you need to register the ODBC-JDBC driver by calling the *forName( )* method from the *Class* class and then calling the *getConnection( )* method from the *DriverManager* class.

The *getConnection( )* method of the DriverManager class attempts to locate the driver that can connect to the database represented by the JDBC URL passed to the *getConnection( )* method.

The JDBC URL:

The JDBC URL is a string that provides a way of identifying a database. A JDBC URL is divided into three parts:

<protocol>:<subprotocol>:<subname>

<subname> is used to identify the database.

A Sample JDBC URL

String url = "jdbc:odbc:MyDataSource";
Class.forName("sun.jdbc.odbc.JdbcOdbcDriver");
Connection con = DriverManager.getConnection(url);

Querying a Database:

Once a connection with the database is established, you can query the database and process the result set. JDBC does not enforce any restriction on the type of SQL statements that can be sent, but as a programmer it is your responsibility to ensure that the database is able to process the statements.

JDBC provides three classes for sending SQL statements to a database. These are:

The Statement Object:

You can create the statement object by calling the *createStatement( )* method from the *Connection* object.

The *PreparedStatement* Object:

You can create the *PreparedStatement* object by calling the *preparedStatement ( )* method from the Connection object. The *PreparedStatement* object contains a set of methods that you can use for sending queries with *INPUT* parameters.

The CallableStatement Object

You can create the *CallableStatement* object by calling *prepareCall( )* method from the *Connection* object. The *CallableStatement* object contains functionality for calling a stored procedure. You can handle both *INPUT* as well as *OUTPUT* parameters using the *CallableStatement* object.

Using the Statement Object

you can use the Statement object to send simple queries to the database as shown in the sample QueryApp program.

Example:

```
// QueryApp.Java

import java.sql. *;

public class QueryApp

{

        public static void main(String arg[ ] )

        {

                try

                {

                  Class.forName("sun.jdbc.odbc.JdbcOdbcDriver");
                  Connection con;
                  Con = DriverManager.getConnection("jdbc:odbc:MyDataSource", "sa"," ");
                  Statement stat = con.createStatement( ) ;
                  stat.executeQuery("select * from tableName");
                }

                catch(Exception e)

                {
                        System.out.println("Error  " + e);
                }

        }

}
```

In the above QueryApp example:

1. The JDBC-ODBC bridge driver is loaded.
2. The Connection object is initialized using the *getConnection( )* method.
3. The Statement object is created using the *createStatement( )* method.
4. Finally, a simple query is executed using the *executeQuery( )* method of the Statement object.

The Statement Object:

The *Statement* object allows you to execute simple queries. It has three methods that can be used for the purpose of querying.

The *executeQuery( )* method executes a simple select query and returns a single *ResultSet* object.

The *execute( )* method executes a SQL statement that may return multiple results.

The ResultSet Object:

The *ResultSet* object provides you with methods to access data from the table. Executing a statement usually generates a *ResultSet* object. It remains a cursor pointing to its current row of data. Initially, the cursor is positioned before the first row. The *next( )* method moves the cursor to the next row. You can access data from the *ResultSet* rows by calling the *getXXX( )* methods, where *xxx* is the data type of the parameter. The following code queries the database and processes the *ResultSet.*

```java
// QueryApp.java

import java.sql.*;
public class QueryApp
{
        public static void main(String args[ ] )
        {
                ResultSet result;
                try
                {
                        Class.forname("sun.jdbc.odbc.JdbcOdbcDriver");
                        Connection con =
                        DriverManager.getConnection("jdbc:odbc:MyDatasource","sa","");
                        Statement stat = con.createStatement( );
                        Result = stat.executeQuery("Select * from TableName");
                        while(result.next())
                        {
                                System.out.println(result.getString(2));
                        }
                }
                catch(Exception e)
                {
                        System.out.println("Error "+e)
                }
        }
}
```

In the above QueryApp example:
1. The ResultSet object is returned by the *executeQuery( )* method.
2. All the rows in the *ResultSet* object are processed using the *next( )* method in a while loop.
3. The values of the second column are retrieved using the *getString( )* method.

The *PreparedStatement* Object:

The *PreparedStatement* object allows you to execute *parameterized* queries. The *PreparedStatement* object is created using the *preparedStatement( )* method of the Connection object.

> *stat = con.preparedStatement("Select * from studentRecord where std_id=?");*

The *preparedStatement( )* method of the Connection object takes an SQL statement as a parameter. The SQL statement can contain *placeholders* that can be replaced by INPUT parameters at runtime.

The '?' symbol is a placeholder that can be replaced by the INPUT parameters at runtime.

Passing INPUT Parameters

Before executing a PreparedStatement object, you must set the value of each '?' parameter. This is done by calling *setXXX( )* method, where *xxx* is the datatype of the parameter.

```
stat.setString(1,pid.getText());
ResultSet result = stat.executeQuery( );
```

Adding Records:

You can use the *executeUpdate( )* method of the Statement object simple INSERT statements.

stat.executeUpdate( ) method is the number of rows affected by the query.

The return value of the *executeUpdate( )* method is the number of rows affected by the query.

```
public void addRecord( )
{
        try
        {
                stat.executeUpdate("Insert publishers values("1020","New Publisher");
        }
        catch(Exception e)
        {

        }
}
```

MODIFYING RECORDS:

You can use the *executeUpdate ( )* method of the Statement object to execute simple UPDATE statements.

stat.executeUpdate("Update <tablename> set <expr> ");

The return value of the executeUpdate ( ) method is the number of rows affected by the query.

```
public void modifyRecord( )
{
        try
        {
                stat.executeUpdate("Update publishers set pub_name='New Publisher' where
                pub_id='1234' ");
        }
        catch(Exception e)
        {

        }
}
```

DELETING RECORDS: You can use the *executeUpdate( )* method of the Statement object to execute simple DELETE statements.

    stat.executeUpdate("delete <tableName>where <expr>");

The return value of the *executeUpdate( )* method is the number of rows affected by the query.

```
public void deleteRecord( )
{
      try
      {
            stat.executeUpdate("delete publishers  where pub_id='1234' ");
      }
      catch(Exception e)
      {

      }
}
```